Who Me? Debt Free?

Who Me? Debt Free?

A Christian's Guide to Living a Debt Free Life

Lucy Vellema

VMI Publishers • Sisters, Oregon

Who Me? Debt Free?

Published by
VMI Publishers
Sisters, Oregon
www.vmipublishers.com

ISBN: 1-933204-71-0
ISBN 13: 978-1-933204-71-0
Library of Congress Control Number: 2008933072

Printed in the USA.

Cover design by Joe Bailen

Dedication

This book is dedicated to my husband, David Vellema. You have been an anchor and a refuge for me in times of uncertainty. I thank God every day for the privilege of being your wife. When God gave you to me, He gave me the very best. I stand in awe of your wisdom, patience, understanding, integrity and perseverance. Your unconditional love and devotion have made me into the woman that I am today. I love you!

To my children Amanda, Allison and Jacob, my three precious treasures. God, through His infinite grace and mercy, has granted me permission to love and raise you. You breathe life and joy into my inmost being. Being your mother is the greatest privilege and reward God has bestowed upon me. My children, you are the love of my life!

TABLE OF CONTENTS

Chapter One

My Childhood

I legally immigrated to the United States with my parents and sister on July 25, 1983 from Bucharest, Romania. I have to include the word "legally" because many people ask me if my family lived in the United States as undocumented immigrants. I, of course, tell them that we arrived with proper documentation. My parents had passports and legal documents which allowed all four of us to be here legally in America. With this being said, you could say that we resembled the typical immigrant family. We did not speak a word of English, were living on welfare, and attempting to make ends meet. In September of 1983, my parents enrolled my sister and me at the local public school, and they also enrolled themselves at the local community college. I was placed in third grade at the age of eight and my sister was placed in first grade at the age of six. My sister and I went to school to learn English, and my parents were also attempting to learn English at the local community college. Within six months, all four of us were able to speak enough English to attempt basic communication.

Life was tough for us as immigrants all around, but the toughest aspect for my family was the finances. The welfare check barely stretched to the end of the month. I remember my parents purchasing several loaves of bread and a five-pound block of cheese on a regular basis in order to feed us. I ate so many grilled cheese sandwiches as a kid that now as an adult I cannot look favorably upon a grilled cheese sandwich! I also remember eating corn flakes cereal as a kid on a regular basis. Sometimes a bowl of corn flakes was our dinner since that was the only other form of nutrition in our home at the time. Therefore, our staple for us kids growing up was a grilled cheese sandwich and cereal since these were the cheapest form of nutrition my parents could provide.

My mom and dad were extremely educated in our native country. My father was a designer engineer and my mother was a registered nurse. When we came to the United States, my parents were informed that they had to become recertified in their fields in order to acquire positions as nurse and an engineer. Basically, the bottom line was that both my parents had to go back to school and start their studies from the very beginning. This was not an easy decision since my dad was forty-three and my mom was thirty-six years old. Besides age being a factor, my parents also had two young daughters to rear. My mom decided to go back to school to renew her nursing credentials and my dad stayed home to raise my sister and me. Life was not easy for us. My mom went to school during the day and then went to work the graveyard shift at the local hospital in order to make ends meet financially. My mom eventually acquired her LVN and then her RN degrees for nursing. We eventually were able to get off welfare since my mom was making more money than the income the welfare check was bringing in. This took place over a ten-year period.

Even though my mom was making just a little bit more money with her nursing credentials, we were still just scraping by. I remember my mom using her credit cards and taking out loans on a regular basis in order for us to make ends meet each month. We were literally living from one paycheck to the next. By no means were we living a lavish lifestyle! We lived in a two-bedroom apartment from the time we came to the US until I went off to college at the age of eighteen. My family lived in an eight-hundred square foot apartment for ten years since this is all my parents could afford to pay. All of our furniture in our apartment had been donated by the local church we were attending. We owned only one car—the oldest and ugliest brown Pinto hatchback you have ever seen! This car was also donated by a generous member in our congregation. I remember my dad having just enough money to put gas in the Pinto every other week. What about car insurance, you ask? In 1984, when we acquired the Pinto, auto insurance was optional. My dad used to place his old Romanian Bible on the Pinto dashboard and say that God was His insurance policy since we were so poor and could not afford to pay for auto insurance. Yes, we were your typical poor immigrant family with very little money and no hope for a brighter future. There were many times growing up when I didn't know whether or not we would lose the roof over our heads and end up homeless on the street. I watched my parents wreak havoc with their finances by taking out loans and using credit cards in order to pay bills and purchase groceries, the bare necessities of life. This was my first introduction to handling finances.

When I turned sixteen, I immediately got a job as a hostess at a local restaurant making minimum wage. I didn't care how much I was making just as long as I was getting a paycheck every two weeks. I didn't know how to manage my money so I just spent it. Most of the money went to buy me clothes and lunch at school. I wanted to fit in so badly with my peers and not stand out like a sore thumb anymore. I had worn hand-me-downs for the last eight years and I was tired of wearing other peoples' clothes. I wanted to wear new and trendy clothing just like my peers were doing. I also was too embarrassed to pack a lunch for school since all of my friends were buying the fast-food hot lunches offered at school. I had learned to live in the moment, from my parents, with my paychecks, and therefore the money I earned was spent faster than I could earn it. I lived for the next paycheck! I guess you can say that I was living to work rather than working to live. I had absolutely no concept of starting a savings account since my parents didn't have one either. For me, each paycheck was about the here and now of spending. Living paycheck to paycheck as a kid taught me that there is no point in saving since my basic needs of food and shelter need to be met today.

During my senior year in high school, I barely saved just enough money ($50) to send in my application to Cal State Long Beach. I was hoped and prayed that I would be accepted at CSULB, because I did not have any more money (nor did my parents) to apply to any other universities. My friends, of course, were applying to seven or eight universities "just in case" they did not get accepted at their prospective university. As the saying goes, I put all of my eggs in one basket. I truly did not know what I would do if I did not get accepted at Long Beach State. By the grace of God, I received a letter from the university stating that I had been accepted for the fall semester. I was ecstatic! The rest of my senior year just flew by. I graduated from high school in June of 1993.

I began attending Cal State Long Beach in August of 1993. I had made the decision that summer to live off-campus with a roommate because it was cheaper than living in the dorms. I loved being on my own! However, I did not expect to have such a tough time making ends meet. My parents were not able to help me out financially, so I had to apply for financial aid in order to pay for tuition at the university. Even with the school loans, I still needed additional money for living expenses. I decided to get a waitressing job. I was going to school during the day and working evenings in order to pay my bills. Living on my own was a lot tougher than I expected. My days consisted of attending class, going to work and studying for my exams. There was no spare time for me to join any sororities or other clubs on campus. However, I did make one exception on Thursday nights. I joined the Campus Crusade for Christ organization on campus. I met wonderful friends and leaders who cheered me on and also encouraged me to persevere through my tough times. It was through this organization that I met my husband David in January of 1996. He was (and still is) a beacon of light for me! He became my best friend and confidant. He coached and guided me through some difficult financial and personal dilemmas I was encountering during this period in my life. Through this process, God impressed upon my heart that this was the man He had designated for me to marry. We obviously did not waste any time. David and I were married the very next year on January 11, 1997. What a blessing! David and I recently celebrated our ten-year anniversary by taking our very first Hawaiian vacation with our two beautiful daughters and our son who was in utero at the time. What a blessing this time together as a family was for all of us!

Chapter Two

Our Journey Begins

If anyone were to ask me eight years into our marriage if I ever thought I could live debt free, my answer would have been, "No way!" I figured that the only way we could ever be debt free was by winning the lottery or having a twice removed aunt dying and leaving us a huge inheritance. These were the only two alternatives I felt that could eliminate the overwhelming burden of debt in which we had buried ourselves. David and I were living paycheck to paycheck and wondering how the next bill would be paid. Every day, as I received mail, I would dread opening up the bills since the amount of debt we owed was enough to make me nauseous. The burden of debt we were responsible for was above and beyond what we were able to afford. We were obviously living beyond our means!

When David and I were married, I brought along with me approximately $15,000 of debt. A large portion of this debt that had accumulated was the result of several student loans I had acquired while completing my bachelor's degree at Long Beach State. David, on the other hand, had been wise with his money and had lived debt free up until we were married. The famous saying, "When you marry someone, you marry their baggage," was definitely true for us. Once we were married the debt no longer enslaved just me, but also my husband. David and I were both working hard to eradicate my student loan debt.

The first seven months of our marriage was financially doable. David was working full-time and I was working part-time at night while attending school during the day. I was desperately trying to finish my bachelor's degree before we even contemplated starting a family. I would write term papers and study for exams from the time I came home from school until I needed to go to work. I was waitressing at night in order to bring in some extra income. With our two incomes we were able to make ends meet between our rent and the debt we owed. We were living conservatively in a one-bedroom apartment near the university I attended. During the summer of 1997, we were surprised to find out that I was pregnant with our first child. I still had one more year left to graduate with a college diploma. I was determined to graduate no matter how hard it would be. I had heard of friends getting pregnant and postponing their college education until later. But for most of these women, I found out, later never came. I didn't want to be another statistic of dropping out of school and never coming back to finish what I had started.

During my pregnancy, my morning sickness became quite unbearable for the next four months. I had to quit my waitressing job because I could no longer walk through the doors of the restaurant without being repulsed by its smells. We were forced to live off of one income with very little money in our savings account. It was tough but bearable. About six months into my pregnancy, we decided that we needed an extra bedroom for the baby. David's parents offered to move us into their rental property (a house) for the same price we were paying for the one-bedroom apartment. This house would be spacious enough for us since it was a two-bedroom home. With the arrival of the baby soon approaching, we were grateful for the additional space. In April of 1998, our first daughter, Amanda, was born, and the next month in May I graduated with my bachelor's degree in social work from Cal State Long Beach. The summer of 1998 was financially tough since we had the added expense of our baby. David and I decided now that I had my bachelor's degree that I had to get a full-time job by September in order not to drown financially.

All summer long I kept searching for a possible job I could get with just my bachelor's degree. During the course of my internships, through the social work program at Long Beach State, I realized that I did not want to work for DCFS (Department of Children and Family Services) as a social worker. I was exposed to a typical social worker's grueling schedule such as long hours, dealing with family crises, removing kids from a potentially dangerous home environment, et cetera. I just knew that this was not the type of job I wanted to occupy after graduation. However, I knew that I really enjoyed working with kids. I spent all summer after graduation contemplating and researching what alternatives were available to me with just a bachelor's degree. In early August of 1998, I felt like I had exhausted all my resources in attempting to find a job. I was just about to give up job hunting and return to waitressing, since that was about the only job I really had mastered over the last five years. A friend had heard of my dilemma and suggested that I apply for a special education teaching position with the local school district. I was somewhat apprehensive about applying for a job I knew nothing about, but I decided to give it a try. Besides, my only other option was waitressing and I was not looking forward to waiting tables with a college degree. I had also accumulated quite a few student loans over the past five years, and my grace period of six months of not having to pay for these loans was shortly coming to an end. I had approximately three months left of my grace period before the student loan bills would be knocking at my door.

I acquired an application from the local school district and filled out the necessary paperwork. I submitted the application somewhat reluctantly to the personnel department. I wasn't to enthusiastic about being called for an interview since I really had no idea what a special education teacher's duties and responsibilities entailed. I was afraid of being asked specific questions regarding this type of position and not knowing the answers. The next day, after submitting the application, I decided that the personnel department must have looked at my resume and realized that I had absolutely no experience working with special education students. I figured that they had disregarded my application altogether.

To my surprise, on the fourth day after submitting my application I was called by the district's human resources department to come in for an interview. Of course I accepted the offer for an interview since no other job prospects were knocking on my door. I began to feel really nervous about the upcoming interview due to my lack of knowledge in regards to this position. I decided to be honest and upfront with the interviewer and let him/her know that I had absolutely no experience working with disabled students.

I showed up at the interview on time and was escorted to the back office where my interview would be taking place. A middle-aged woman with short black hair introduced herself and instructed me to sit down. After the formal introductions were completed, I almost immediately "spilled my guts" regarding my lack of experience. I obviously know now that this was not the smartest way to begin an interview. The interviewer thoughtfully considered my forward reply and then began to ask me questions regarding the social work internships I had posted on my resume. I began to express to her how much I enjoyed helping others and that I'd realized, through the internships, that I really enjoyed working with kids. I believe that the interviewer must have seen a raw willingness and a determination on my part to truly want to help others. I was informed by the end of the interview that several principals would be contacting me regarding various special education positions at their school sites.

I left the interview feeling somewhat hopeful regarding my prospects for a job with the school district, even if it was for a job I really didn't know much about. I was young, twenty-three years old, and willing to utilize my skills in whatever environment and capacity I was placed. The next day I was contacted by a principal who ended up hiring me at his school site for an intermediate learning handicapped position. This position, I was informed, entailed working with fourth and fifth grade students who had learning disabilities which inhibited them from acquiring the academic curriculum. The principal, furthermore, told me that these kids were basically regular happy-go-lucky students who had severe difficulties processing and retaining academic information. I was then hired by the district as a long-term substitute for a period of three-and-a-half months. I worked in this position from September until December when the kids were off for Christmas break. These three-and-a-half months were the most rewarding times I had spent with a group of kids, but this was also the most challenging position I had ever held.

These students taught me to never take anything for granted, especially when it came to using my brain. The frustration and tears these kids shed on a daily basis moved me deeply. Their ability to retain simple concepts in the academic context was almost non-existent. Each child's degree of severity obviously varied for each one of them. However, each one struggled daily to remember the process of how to solve a simple math problem or how to decode a particular word they had been learning continuously since kindergarten. Life for these kids was a daily struggle to achieve success with the basics in academics. These kids taught me how to appreciate the simple pleasures in life. A hug and a welcoming smile was enough to make their day a beautiful journey to enjoy!

This first long-term substitute teaching job allowed me to see how much I enjoyed being in the educational arena, and it also gave me the opportunity to bring home a decent income (when compared to waitressing). Although I was making more money now, it still was not enough to help cover the expenses we were incurring each month.

Each month, when the paychecks came, David and I would decide which bills we would pay first, which ones needed to wait and which ones we were going to consolidate for that month on another credit card. It seemed that our financial situation was a juggling act of which bills would be paid and which ones would be postponed until the next month since we just did not have enough funds to cover all of our expenses. I decided that I needed a more permanent position with the school district and also a position which paid more than what I was making then. Thus began my search for higher education.

Chapter Three

Drowning in Debt

I realized that as a teacher my day was scheduled and outlined with a specific curriculum I had to follow. I wasn't able to go into detail regarding some of the negative behavior characteristics I had noticed some of the kids were exhibiting. I wanted to be able to offer these kids behavior modification techniques in order for them to avoid getting into trouble at school and also to improve their home environment. I wanted to be involved with the kids from a holistic perspective, as I had been taught throughout my social work program. I began to explore and inquire about other possible positions within a school that would allow me to work with school-age kids and their parents with various behavioral, emotional and/or social dilemmas they might be experiencing.

I had befriended the school counselor at the school I was assigned to for that first teaching job. She began to discuss with me the program she had gone through in order to become a school counselor. I wasn't so sure that I wanted to go back to school so soon. It had only been six months since I had graduated with my bachelor's degree. I was so tired of going to school since it had taken me five long years to accomplish my bachelor's! However, by November of 1998, I had made up my mind to attend the counseling program. After I researched the program, I then signed up with the University of La Verne to complete my school counseling credentials along with my master's in school counseling. I began attending class in January of 1999.

While going to school at night, I was also working during the day as a substitute teacher. I worked until the middle of June when school was out for summer vacation. It was tough working by day, going to school at night, having a one-year-old daughter at home and maintaining a marriage. No wonder I was so exhausted each night as I lay my head down on my pillow. My exhaustion was compounded when I found out that I was also pregnant with our second daughter in early June of that year (1999). I was so glad that I had fulfilled my contract as a substitute teacher for that year, since my morning sickness was escalating. Looking back now, I honestly do not know how I made it through that year except by the grace of God!

The following year on February 7, 2000, our second daughter, Allison, was born. I laboriously continued with school by writing term papers, taking exams, and finishing my thesis. I felt increasingly overwhelmed by my responsibilities. Between my almost two-year-old, my newborn baby, school and home, I wasn't sure I would graduate by the deadline. I decided then that I was not super-mom and enlisted my dad to come and help me out from the bind I was in. He would come over and take our oldest daughter out to the park, on walks, and anywhere else she wanted to be entertained. I would then feed my youngest daughter and place her back in her bassinet while I returned to typing away at my thesis. In the evenings when my husband would come home from work, I would also enlist his services of child-care while I typed for another two to three hours at night. This cycle of my dad coming over, feeding the baby, late nights and typing continuously went on for approximately one month until I had completed my thesis. By August of 2000, I had completed my studies and received my diploma for my master's degree accompanied by my school counseling credential. I will forever be indebted to my father and my husband for supporting me through this endeavor.

By September of 2000, I had received a job offer for a school counseling position from the same school district I had worked for previously. Some of my duties and responsibilities included counseling kids for emotional, social and behavioral dilemmas; disciplining students for inappropriate behavior; coordinating testing schedules for the state mandated achievement tests; testing students for various assessments; working with parents to modify inappropriate behavior their children were exhibiting; assisting teachers with challenging behaviors in the classroom environment; et cetera. I loved working with the students, teachers, administrators and parents in the educational arena.

I worked as a school counselor for the next five years. However, after working for three years as a school counselor, I decided to go back to school for my administrative credential. As a counselor, I found myself at times taking on administrative type of duties just like my principal was faced with. I decided that by going back to school, I could be better equipped to handle myself if I had more training in the administrative realm. By August 2003, I again enlisted myself with the University of La Verne to work on my administrative credential. I was informed that this was a year long program. I had intended to only get my administrative credential, but about halfway through the program I was informed that I could receive a second master's degree if I just added one more additional class to my schedule. This class was the thesis portion of the curriculum. I went ahead and completed this last class of the program and graduated in August 2004 with my administrative credential and my second master's in educational management.

After I had finished my second master's and a second credential, David and I found ourselves with thirty thousand dollars of combined student loans. These student loans were in addition to our first mortgage. We also had a ten thousand dollar credit card debt and also a $15,000 second mortgage we were carrying. Our total debt, not including our primary monthly mortgage, was calculated at $55,000. We were in over our heads with all the debt we had accumulated! You would have thought that as two educated individuals we would have been able to resolve our debt dilemma. Unfortunately, we did not know where to begin attacking our burden of debt. David and I were having a tough time paying our $2300 primary mortgage each month much less attempting to pay the other incoming bills. What makes matters worse is that we were both working full-time and making a little over $100,000 per year, and we still were struggling to pay our bills. It is sad to say that for the first eight years of our married life we were literally living paycheck to paycheck. There were many days when we would contemplate which bills we were not going to pay for that month in order to have enough money left over to buy the bare necessities such as groceries. The next month we would again reevaluate and pay only the past due notices and the bills we did not pay the previous month. At one point, we were so desperate for money that we even took out a loan against David's 401(K) retirement account. We knew that this was not a smart financial decision because not only were we taxed on the additional income, but we were also penalized at the highest taxable rate by Uncle Sam for dipping into David's retirement account. We were taxed twice on the money we borrowed! What a grave mistake we made! I guess desperation forced us to make some pretty irrational financial decisions. The cycle of debt, unfortunately, perpetuated itself month after month in our family's life.

David and I would daily ask ourselves what we were doing wrong with our finances since we could never seem to catch up with our bills. We were both working full-time and still not able to make ends meet. We decided to try debt consolidation in order to alleviate some of the financial burden we were carrying. David, being the finance guy, told me that we were only moving our debt around and not really resolving the debt problem. I didn't care. I just wanted some breathing room from all the piling debt we had accumulated. So we tried debt consolidation. We decided to refinance our mortgage in order to pay off the student loan debt. At the time of the refinance, we were only able to consolidate the $30,000 school loans because this is all the equity we had accumulated from our home. I was happy just to alleviate some of the burden of debt we were under. So instead of taking us seven to ten years to pay off the debt, we decided to add the debt to our mortgage which will now take us thirty years to pay off. How smart was that? I guess I was only attempting to alleviate our short-term financial crises and not thinking really of the long-term effects of debt consolidation. Here is some important information on this concept of debt consolidation.

Chapter Four

Debt Consolidation

Debt is like a disease to those suffering from it. Like a disease, debt never really goes away. In fact, it persists and persists and it never truly gets better until action is taken to eliminate the debt. A person's debt, like a disease, causes a great deal of suffering and pain. Those suffering from debt will feel a combination of emotions such as shame, depression, embarrassment, anger and anxiety. Due to these overwhelming emotions, many people will try to alleviate their suffering by attempting to temporarily eradicate their debt through a debt consolidation loan. This type of loan has become the "loan of choice" for many debtors seeking a temporary haven.

In our debt-ridden society, being in debt is no longer viewed as an unsolvable dilemma. Debt consolidation has become an increasingly popular way for people to deal with their escalating debts. Debt consolidation mortgages are among the main methods that debtors use to manage their financial affairs. Debt consolidation involves swapping all of your individual debts for one large debt with only one monthly payment. Therefore, by consolidating your debts you will end up with one larger debt which is repaid over a longer period of time. Debt consolidation is not a cheap option. Most of these loans will ultimately cost more in interest over the entire duration of the loan than if you had taken the time and paid off the loans in their own time.

Haven't we all heard of debt-consolidation commercials advertising a "quick-fix" to our money problems? These commercials go something like this: "Are you 30, 60 or 90 days late with your mortgage payment? Are you also behind on your car loan? Do you have several credit cards that are completely maxed out? Do you live in constant dread that someone will soon come knocking on your door to claim their money? Are collection agencies calling you relentlessly? Do you feel as if all the money you are earning goes towards paying the high interest rates on all your loans rather than actually paying off the principal of each loan? Then a debt consolidation loan is what you need!" These advertisements give the impression that a consumer's financial problems will be alleviated if they get debt consolidation loans. But do you really think that a debt consolidation loan will fix all your financial problems? Most people think that a debt consolidation is the answer to their prayers. However, this is the farthest thing from the truth. Like most people, I also thought this type of loan would be the answer to our chaotic financial situation. Our debt consolidation loan alleviated some of the burden from the debt we were carrying, but in the long run it only made matters worse. Therefore, a debt consolidation loan might help alleviate some of the short-term pressures from bills, but it will not fix the financial crisis.

To people drowning in debt, like us, a debt consolidation loan looks a lot like a lifesaver. However, agreeing to such a loan without understanding it completely could be a serious mistake. There are some facts about debt consolidation that we as consumers may want to "lend" an ear to. It is important to keep in mind that a debt consolidation loan does not "fix" the financial predicament we find ourselves in. At best, it is a 'temporary fix" to our finances because it gives us a false sense of relief from our bills. In reality, debt consolidation can actually multiply your debts. As consumers, we need to watch out for sky-high rates, hidden fees, costly add-ons and damage to our credit rating.

The trouble with debt consolidation loans is twofold. First, this type of borrowing typically does nothing to solve the problem that got the consumer into trouble. This "problem" is called overspending. *More borrowing does not alleviate the debt problem, but rather it perpetuates the cycle of debt.* Secondly, loans can be far more expensive than the debt they're designed to pay off. These loans are usually full of hidden fees, expensive insurance and other profit-boosters for the lenders. So, on top of the debt one has already accumulated, they will throw on more debt (the cost of the loan) to their already heavy burden of debt in order to consolidate their bills. Huh? Will this insane cycle of debt ever come to an end?

There are four types of loans that are typically used to consolidate debt: home-equity lending (secured); personal (unsecured) lending; home refinancing (secured); and credit cards (unsecured). Home-equity lending or line of credit allows the consumer to borrow against the value of his/her home. Personal lending could be backed by the consumer's home, cars or other collateral, but essentially the bank relies on the borrower's promise to pay. If the borrower does not pay back the loan then the bank may go after the collateral used against the loan. Personal loans offer interest rates of 14 to 15 percent for individuals with good credit. People with heavy debts or troubled credit will usually pay higher interest rates. They can be as high as 18 to 21 percent. Those who choose a personal loan may also face upfront fees as much as ten percent of the loan amount. Home refinancing gives the borrower one large bill to pay rather than numerous bills to pay each month. Refinancing gives the home owner a false sense of relief from the heavy debt burden. He/she has taken a debt that could have probably been paid off over ten to fifteen years, and now has extended that debt over a thirty- or forty-year period. Most people who use this "temporary fix" method usually get right back into debt because they have not solved their root problem: spending money they do not have. Credit cards are the fourth way people attempt to consolidate their debt. This method could be beneficial to those who consolidate their debt on a zero percent credit card offer and are able to pay off their loan before the interest rate skyrockets. However, most people do not end up paying off the loan before the interest rate rises, and some people actually begin to miss their payments while they are on that zero percent interest. Part of the contingency offer of credit card companies is that people make their payments on time. In the fine print of that credit card agreement it states that if you are late with your payment then the interest rate automatically jumps to 21 percent or higher depending on the credit card company.

If borrowers can secure a low-rate, low-cost loan and pay their debt off faster than they may otherwise, then debt consolidation makes sense. Too often, though, consumers look for lower payments rather than lower costs. Lower payments usually mean it will take you longer to pay off your debt and thus inflate the total amount you ultimately will pay for that loan. Therefore, a debt consolidation loan may not always be the answer to your finances. Perhaps you may be able to lower your interest rate if you simply ask your creditors. If you have good credit, your credit card companies may be willing to lower your rate. It never hurts to ask. If the representative says "No" then ask them to transfer you to his/her supervisor. If the supervisor's answer is still "NO," then tell him that he will be losing your business to another company which is currently offering you a zero percent introductory offer. Sometimes credit card companies will want to keep your business and therefore they will oblige to your request and lower your interest rate. Other times the answer will be "No" no matter whom you talk to. Then you need to decide if a balance transfer to a lower interest rate is right for your financial dilemma. A note of caution when transferring balances: use this tactic with moderation because if you apply for too many credit cards then your credit will be negatively impacted.

Chapter Five

The Cycle of Debt

After our debt consolidation, David and I felt as if the burden of debt had been lifted. This feeling, however, was only temporary. David and I had not treated our root problem of overspending which got us in debt in the first place. Both of us liked to purchase nice things for ourselves and our kids. However, in David's defense, I do have to say that I was notorious for opening up new department store credit cards to purchase clothing for myself and the kids. I loved to shop! Every time I would open up a new credit card, I would tell myself that I was actually saving money (the 10 percent deduction when a new credit card is opened) and that we would be able to pay off the balance at the end of the month. I knew deep down, though, that we really would not be able to cover the additional credit card balance at the end of the month. I was in denial about our financial crisis. When I would finally come home from my shopping sprees, I would hide some of the purchases from David because I knew how upset he would be with me. I knew that my reckless spending habits were ruining our marriage, but I just couldn't help myself. I found peace and happiness when I shopped. I felt that shopping gave me comfort and relief from the overwhelming burden I felt at our financial predicament. These joyous feelings, however, were only temporary. Reality soon set in on my drive home from my shopping extravaganza, and my feelings of sadness, depression and hopelessness would resurface. I was also not looking forward to facing the music when I got home. I hated hiding things from David, because we had always had a pretty straightforward and honest relationship. I hid purchases from David because I was afraid of how angry he would be with me, since I knew that my frivolous spending was putting us further into debt than we already were. Of course, at the end of the month we would have to borrow money from another credit card to pay off the new card. To use an analogy of our behavior—it is like we were robbing Peter to pay Paul. What a financial mess we were in! To sum up our life in a nutshell, we dressed with clothes paid for with credit cards and we walked on financed carpet in our mortgaged house. We realized that we owned nothing and we were prisoners of our debt. This vicious cycle of debt was ruining our marriage and forcing us to fall deeper into debt.

David and I were not only overspending and not living within our means, but we also did not allocate enough funds for other larger expenses. Some of these bills included our car insurance; the car breaking down; Christmas present et cetera. We began charging our way again into debt since we could not pay for these bills. The tendency for David and I was to keep on borrowing on credit since we could not save enough money of our own to pay for these expenses. And why should we when the process of borrowing was so easy? There were several credit card companies who were willing to throw cash at us on a weekly basis with such low interest rates on the credit card offers we would receive in the mail. Now we know that this is their tactic to trap us for life in the cycle of credit card debt.

The cycle of debt is an epidemic disease in our society today. If this disease is not treated, it will grow into a very serious problem. The amount of unsecured debt (mostly credit card balances) is rising at an astronomical rate. Many people today are taking on debt beyond what they can afford to repay. The cause of the rapid increase in unsecured debt is due primarily to people simply borrowing left and right in order to financially survive. They are barely able to keep their "heads above the water" financially, and the only way they know how to manage their finances is by borrowing money from one card to pay off another credit card. What a vicious and never ending cycle this becomes! Many are losing sleep and worried sick about how they are going to get out of this financial hole. Unfortunately, people today have overextended themselves financially more than ever before. If there is a change in their circumstances, such as losing their jobs, getting divorced, becoming ill, et cetera, their personal situations are that much more unstable. Experts estimate that many people are about two paychecks away from financial disaster. Are you financially prepared to handle an unexpected event? How will you cover your unsecured debt if you are unable to bring in a paycheck every two weeks? I hope the answer is not "using my credit cards" because you will further perpetuate this vicious cycle of debt in your life. The following questions force you to take a hard look at your present financial circumstances and evaluate the degree to which you have succumbed to the cycle of debt. Do any of these questions apply to you and your family?

1. Are you losing sleep at night over your finances?
2. Have you spent up to your limit on more than one credit card?
3. Do you regularly exceed your bank overdraft to the extent that you are not in credit when your wages are paid into the bank?
4. Do you keep some of your spending habits secret from your spouse?
5. Do you simply leave mail unopened if you think it contains demands for payment?
6. Do you have to borrow money to cope with a financial emergency such as your car breaking down?
7. Do you use credit cards to pay for everyday expenses such as groceries?
8. Have debt collectors contacted you about an unpaid bill or bills?
9. Do you frequently have arguments at home about money?
10. Do you go shopping to relieve the depression caused by being in debt?

If you answered yes to at least two of the above questions, I believe that you need to admit to yourself that your finances are controlling you and that you are perpetuating the vicious cycle of debt in your life. All ten of these scenarios were drafted from the experiences David and I went through due to our overwhelming burden of debt. We did not know what to do or where to start alleviating the cycle of debt we found ourselves in on a monthly basis.

To make matters worse, I decided not to work full-time anymore. I dropped down to a part-time counseling position with the school district in order for me to spend more time with our daughters. This decision, of course, did not help our financial predicament in any way. Our financial burden was becoming so overwhelming that we felt that we were drowning in our debt with no way of ever becoming debt free. We were tired of always working, barely seeing our kids and never making ends meet. We decided that we did not want to live like this any longer. David and I were determined to make the necessary changes in order to eradicate our debt.

As Christians, David and I believed that God wanted us to be free of debt and independent in making financial decisions rather than to be enslaved by debt. There are two Bible verses that spoke volumes to us regarding the financial burden we were faced with. One of those verses was Proverbs 22:7 (NIV). In this verse, the wise King Solomon wrote, "The rich rule over the poor, and the borrower is servant to the lender." We were tired of being servants to our lenders! We felt tied to our debt like a ball and chain. Another Bible verse we both took to heart was Romans 13:8. It states, "Let no debt remain outstanding, except the continuing debt to love one another . . ." There are two messages in this verse that God had imprinted upon our hearts. One was to ensure that we do not carry any debt to our name and the second is to continuously love each other. Well, we obviously were not obeying the first command since we were carrying over $50,000 of debt. And we definitely were not even close to the second part of that verse since we were having difficulties loving each other the way God had intended for us to do. David and I were constantly arguing and blaming each other for the financial crisis we were in. Neither one of us wanted to take responsibility for the financial predicament we found ourselves in. Due to the constant arguing and blaming we experienced on a daily basis, our marriage was in jeopardy. At one point, we began to discuss the possibility of divorce. However, we knew deep within our souls that God did not approve of divorce and we decided against this idea.

David and I began to focus on ways in which we could make sense of our financial crisis. We realized that as long as we owed people money, they owned us. At that moment we made ourselves a promise that we would never be this vulnerable financially again. David and I had to find a way out of this debilitating debt. We began to make some drastic changes to our finances in order to survive financially. The first step towards analyzing our financial predicament was to create a workable budget that would fit our needs.

Chapter Six

Budgeting 101

David and I sat down together and began developing a realistic budget for our family. David created a simple Excel budget on our computer which included our income and expenses. Being the finance guy in our family, David began to categorize our income, spending habits, utilities, mortgage, debt, et cetera. Hard to believe, but up to this point we had not developed any sort of budget. David came up with this reasonable budget which he felt we could stick to. The following budget represents the categories to which we allocated our funds. We wanted to get a visual picture of where our money was being spent.

The budget David created has the titles of "monthly budget amount," "monthly actual amount" and "difference." These three columns would serve as a gauge for us to see the amount allocated, amount actually spent and the difference between the two. David and I knew that we were overspending in some categories, but were unsure exactly by how much extra we were spending. The "difference" section of the budget would inform us of where excess money was frivolously being spent. This budget setup forced us to tighten our financial reigns. After the budget was created, we began to track our spending over several months to see where our money was going. We realized that this was the only way to create order out of the chaotic financial mess in which we found ourselves.

Category	Monthly Budget Amount	Monthly Actual Amount	Difference
Income			
Wages & Bonuses			
Expenses			
Mortgage			
Homeowners Insurance			
Property Taxes			
Home Repairs/Improvements			
Utilities			
Electricity			
Water and Trash			
Gas			
Telephone (land line & cell)			
Food			
Groceries			
Eating Out			
Family Obligations			
Child Care			
Transportation			
Car Payments			
Gas			
Car Repairs/Maintenance			
Auto Insurance			
Debt Payments			
Credit Cards			
Student Loans			
Other Loans			
Entertainment			
Cable			
Movies			
Hobies			
Vacations			
Pets			
Food			
Grooming, Boarding & Vet Bills			
Clothing			
Children			
Mom & Dad			
Investment & Savings			
IRA or 401 (K)			
Stocks/Bonds/Mutual Funds			
College Fund			
Savings			
Emergency Fund			
Tithe			
Miscellaneous			
Household Products, Toiletries			
Gifts			
Grooming (hair, make-up, etc.)			
Misc. Expenses			
Total Investments & Expenses			

As you can see, a budget is an essential tool to one's finances. A pilot would never fly a plane without a flight plan. Yet all too often, people spend their money with no clear plan for how they will get where they want to go financially. Most of us view budgets as a necessary evil at best and something to be avoided at worst. However, a budget should be a guide and not a constraint. A realistic and workable budget is nothing more than your plan for how to use your financial resources wisely and effectively. Therefore, a budget allows you to put your money where it is most needed so that your finances will head in the right direction. Creating a reasonable budget lets you control your finances instead of it controlling you. A budget is an integral tool to your finances!

The first step in taking control of your finances is to track your expenses, which invariably means controlling your expenses. Controlling your financial affairs requires a realistic and workable budget. I know that for many people the word "budget" has a negative connotation. Don't think of "budget" as financial handcuffs, but rather as a means to achieve your financial dream of becoming debt free. You owe it to yourself to abandon the chains of bondage that are keeping you enslaved to your debt.

If you are unsure of how to draft a budget, use our budget and adjust it to your needs. The budget categories should be tailored to the expenses you have so that you can create a workable budget. For example, if you do not have any pets then you will not need a category for this expense. However, if you commute to work via metro then you would need to include this expense in your budget. There are basic categories every one of us will have in our budgets such as housing, utilities, and food, but we all have expenses that are unique to our own personal situations. Do not try to fit your spending into someone else's categories, because you are doomed to fail before you even begin. A successful budget will include categories that reflect the way you actually spend your money. The idea of a budget is to become more aware of where your money is going so that you can make conscious decisions about spending.

After you have tracked your actual spending for several months, you will be better able to identify where you can make the necessary cuts and adjustments to your budget in order to start paying off debt and begin saving for the future. Many people do not have a vivid picture of where their money is being spent until they begin tracking their spending habits. After tracking their spending, most people are surprised to find how much money they are actually allocating in certain categories. Once this revelation is discovered, then most people begin to make the necessary changes in order to reallocate their money in the proper avenues. For example, if you tracked your spending over several months and you begin to see a pattern of overspending in the clothes category, then you would take the extra funds from the clothes category and apply it to the credit card balance you owe in order to pay off more debt. Remember that you cannot begin to control your money until you really know how much you have and where it is being spent.

Now that you see the benefits of creating a budget, you are probably wondering if you need to go and spend hundreds of dollars on some fancy software. Absolutely not! You do not need to invest in expensive software in order to do a budget. Many banks are now offering free PC banking and free personal finance software. You simply use your bank's web-based banking and download the checks that have cleared your account and place them directly into your personal finance software. Then you can indicate an expense category for each check. You can then do a basic comparison of budget versus actual expenses by category. Then print your personal financial statements which show your net income and net worth. It is a great visual aid to track your expenses!

If you desire to purchase a personal finance software program for your checkbook and expense tracking, here are some of the most popular software programs: Quicken, MS Money and MoneyDance. Please keep in mind that whether you use a sophisticated personal finance software or a couple of pieces of paper and a pencil, the most important thing to remember is that you need to get on the road to financial freedom by starting a budget today. Do not procrastinate any longer! The sooner you get a handle on your spending the quicker you become in charge of your finances, rather than letting your finances control you. Aren't you tired of letting your finances dictate who you are? Take charge of your life by controlling your financial journey! You CAN write your own positive financial journey rather than letting your finances dictate your life.

Once you have the budgeting process in place, take an in-depth look at your largest spending categories. Begin to brainstorm about different ways to reduce your spending in specific categories. I assure you that if you persevere and stick to this budgeting process, you will begin to see a pattern in your spending, which in turn will allow you to identify areas where frivolous spending takes place. You will be able to make more discretionary purchases because you are in control of your money and not the other way around. Therefore, once you realize where the extra money is being spent, you will be more conscious about putting that extra cash towards paying off your credit cards or building your savings. Cutting costs where frivolous spending occurs can be challenging, but the outcome can be very rewarding as you begin to see progress being made with your financial endeavors.

Chapter Seven

Frivoulous Spending

Are you making "cents" of your finances? Well, David and I were desperately attempting to make "cents' of our financial predicament by creating a realistic budget and cutting costs where frivolous spending was taking place. Through this process we began to slowly untangle the financial web we had created.

A budget is the first and most important step you can take towards putting your money to work for you instead of being controlled by it. Many of us think that we know exactly where our money goes each and every day. But do we really know? That small cup of coffee or newspaper or snack we purchase adds up over the months and adds up even bigger over an entire year. If we are really honest with ourselves and calculate these small expenditures over an entire year, we may be surprised at how much we frivolously spend on these items. Here are some examples of habits you may splurge on that add up to big money over 365 days.

Habit	Daily Cost	Yearly Cost
Daily Cup of Coffee	$2	$730
1 Pack of Cigarettes/day	$6	$2190
Lunch Take-out 5 days/week	$5 (5x5=25x52weeks/year)	$1300
1 Movie @ Theatres/week	$9.00	$432

These are just average costs for these habits. Depending on the store you purchase a particular item, it could cost you less or even more for the habit of choice. For example, if you go to McDonalds to purchase your coffee, it will cost you less than two dollars. However, if you only go to a coffee shop such as Starbucks, then you will pay more for your cup of coffee each day. Also, the yearly cost for lunch is based on a twelve-month calendar year. You can adjust this amount depending on the number of days you are required to work. You are the only one who knows what you are paying for your habit each day, and therefore you can calculate what your habit is costing you on a yearly basis. You will be amazed at how much money you spend on your habit of choice!

I am not saying that you no longer can enjoy a cup of coffee or eating out, but what I am trying to say is that these "habits" can become really expensive once you calculate the yearly cost. One example of trimming these costs could be to brew your own cup of coffee three times a week and enjoy a store bought coffee the other two days a week. Another example on how to save is to pack yourself a lunch three days a week while still enjoying eating out the other two days of the week. Also, how about going to the movies every other week? You will still enjoy the theatre experience twice a month. The other two weeks of the month you can rent a movie. You can either go to a traditional store to rent your movies for about $4.50 a movie or you can get a better deal by renting movies through a machine at your local grocery store. Please let me explain. In my neighborhood at the local grocery store (Ralph's), my husband found a machine that dispenses movies to rent. I love this machine because my family and I can rent movies (even new releases) for just $1. Can you believe it? I can rent adult and kids movies for just one dollar! Unbelievable! I was in shock when my husband told me about this new technology. When renting the DVDs, we have to remember to return them by 7:00pm the next day. If we are late in returning the DVDs, then we are charged $1 for every day that it is not returned by 7:00pm. However, if we do not return the DVD within fourteen days, then we will be charged $35 plus tax for the rented movie. We definitely do not mind the extra trip (three-minute drive) to return the DVD because we know that we are getting a great deal for our money! The way the machine works is that it has a screen, kind of like an ATM, that displays the movies which are available to rent. I scroll through all the movies to pick out a movie we want to watch and then I select my desired movie. It will then ask me to swipe my credit card. My card is charged $1.08—a dollar for the movie and eight cents for tax. Once my credit card information is processed then the machine will dispense the DVD of choice. It takes approximately one to two minutes for the entire transaction to be completed. It is fast, simple and CHEAP!!! For our family, it sure beats going to the local store to rent one movie for over four dollars! If you want to know if such a machine is available in your neighborhood, or you just want more information regarding this new technology of renting DVD's, then log on to the following website: www.thenewrelease.com. Here's a phone number for you to contact as well: 1-800-518-1574. I also noticed at my local Wal-Mart, that there is another company that has chosen the same concept when it comes to renting DVDs. The company is called RedBox and you can access their information at www.redbox.com or by calling 1-866-redbox3. Go ahead and check out this new and innovative way of watching DVD's. There is no penalty for investigating this resource. Your wallet will thank you!

These are just a few things you can do to save a few extra hundred dollars every year. These small changes may not seem to impact your financial predicament in that moment, but over time as you track your spending you will notice that there is more money in your account then you anticipated. Don't think of what you are missing by not having that extra lunch or seeing that extra movie. Think of it as gaining another method of enjoying your time. For example, instead of eating lunch out you can make it a working lunch where you complete a task or project for your boss that you just have not been able to get to. While you are eating your nutritious lunch you packed, you are also accomplishing a goal at work. Depending on your job, you might be able to reward yourself by leaving a half-hour early from work since you were so dedicated and completed that particular task or project.

As you can see, every penny saved adds up to big money. Budgeting gives you a black and white picture of where your money is being spent, and it also enables you to cut the frivolous spending habits that trickle their way into your wallet. A budget, therefore, allows you to begin building a financial safety net in order to prevent financial disasters caused by catastrophic illnesses or other personal tragedies. Many experts state that the average household is only two paychecks away from financial disaster. Do you want your family to become another financial statistic? Of course NOT! Take charge of your financial endeavors before your finances dictate how you lead your life. Therefore, implementing a budget, getting a handle on your spending, and saving for the future allow you to avoid using your credit cards and falling deeper into debt.

After you have established your budget, then you need to set financial goals. What are your financial goals? Are you saving for a down payment on a home, starting a college fund for your kids, buying a new car, planning for retirement, paying off credit card debt, or saving for a trip to Hawaii? Setting financial goals are practical steps anyone could start off with in beginning to prioritize one's budget. Therefore, a good budget has built in short-term, mid-term and long-term financial goals. By setting these financial goals, you are able to plan and allocate your money in the proper avenues so that you are not tempted to use money borrowed on credit. Being intentional about following your short-, mid- and long-term goals will keep you from falling into the credit card trap. You cannot afford to be reckless any longer with your finances. You need these financial goals to pave your path towards becoming debt free. This financial endeavor, therefore, requires commitment, discipline and hard work on your part.

Chapter Eight

Setting Financial Goals

To get where you want to go in life, it is important to decide in advance how you will get there. Goals help you decide how you will reach your destination. Goals are signs on the highway to your future. They serve as your road map to success. Setting financial goals is the first step to developing an effective spending plan. Without goals you may be dissatisfied with where your life is going and how you are utilizing your resources. When you write down your financial goals, you will increase your possibility of reaching them. Writing down your goals forces you to decide whether you are willing to spend the time, effort and money necessary to achieve your goals. Just the act of writing down your financial goals can set the process in motion.

Writing down your financial goals creates the road map to your success. There are three financial goals you need to focus on: short-term goals, mid-term goals and long-term goals. Short-term goals are accomplished between a week and a few months, but no longer than a year. For example, saving to buy school clothes or saving for a family vacation is considered a short-term goal. Mid-term goals are accomplished in one to five years. These goals may include saving to buy a new car or paying off a credit card balance. Long-term goals are achieved in five years or more. These goals involve big expenses such as purchasing a house, sending your kids to college and building a financial safety net for retirement. By setting these three types of goals, you begin to paint a vivid picture of how you will choose to allocate your financial resources.

Financial goals will help you to determine where your money will go. Financial goals need to be specific, realistic and measurable. For example, writing the goal, "I want to be debt free" is extremely vague and overwhelming. What if you are buried in $75,000 worth of debt and you are barely scraping by financially? How will you achieve this financial goal? You have to elaborate and specify exactly how you will achieve this monumental goal in order to have a more defined image of what your end result will be. For example, the goal may include the following details: "I will stop my frivolous spending by creating a budget; I will be debt free in five years; and I will seek some guidance from a credit counselor who will assist me in creating a budget which I can follow." There is now a more realistic, specific and measurable set of instructions to work towards. Can you now close your eyes and visualize the process I just described? The more information you give yourself, the more defined the final outcome becomes. By being specific about your goals, you can direct your energy toward achieving your goals. Therefore, by setting financial goals, you will be better prepared when life throws you some curve balls. Believe me; life has a way of throwing you some unexpected curve balls such as your car breaking down or your spouse getting laid off from work. These unfortunate events happen to all of us at one time or another; and it is up to us to be intentional about the financial choices we make during these difficult circumstances. For example, if your car breaks down, will you fix it or will you just buy a new car? What about if your spouse loses his job? Will you do without some things or will you continue spending by using your credit cards? When times like these come and you are faced with a financial predicament, you will need to ask yourself this question: "Will this decision bring me closer to my financial goals or further from my goals?" If the answer is "closer to" then you know that you are making the right decision. But if the answer is "further from" then you know what you should not be doing. If you follow this process, you will be on your way to achieving success with the financial goals you have set for yourself. There is no greater joy than seeing your plan of action yielding a positive outcome with your finances.

To achieve your financial goals, you must start today and no longer postpone goal setting until tomorrow. The keys to achieving your financial goals are commitment and discipline. You must be committed to the financial goals you set and you must practice discipline. You must be willing to defer things that would be nice now for the things you really want to financially achieve. Setting financial goals and following through on them will yield some wonderful financial benefits such as guidance, peace of mind, direction, and a vision for your financial future. No one but you can put your plan into action. Therefore, do not procrastinate any longer—get started today! Your future will thank you for being proactive with your finances today.

Earning money is only half the equation for achieving financial independence. Effectively putting your money to work for you is equally important. The size of your household income matters when you are attempting to eliminate debt, but more importantly, how you manage the money you have will determine how you live today and in the future. Managing your money effectively will help you meet your short-term, mid-term and long-term goals. These goals are crucial to achieving financial independence. Short-term, mid-term and long-term goals are the signs on the highway for your financial future. These highway signs guide and lead you on your journey toward becoming debt free. These goals also assist you with any financial detours you may be tempted to take. By having these three basic goals in place, you will be empowered to take control of your finances.

There are many benefits to paying off your debt and achieving financial independence. One of the benefits of financial independence is that you will be able to determine and shape your own destiny. You will be able to dictate the path in life you want to take in order to accomplish other dreams and desires that have been placed on hold as a result of your debt. For example, have you always wanted to visit Europe, or have you had a passion for missions and wanted to work as a missionary in Africa? Well, now that you are no longer tied down by your debt, you are free to make these decisions. Another benefit of financial independence is that you will have a truer sense of your identity since you no longer have the label of debtor attached to it. Without this repulsive label dragging you down, you will be able to fully harness your economic power and therefore guarantee full returns on your financial endeavors. There are so many more benefits to becoming debt free such as: no more late fees; no more finance charges; no more being depressed all the time; no more not having money in your pocket; no more sleepless nights, et cetera. The benefits you will reap from the elimination of your debt will empower and energize you to achieve other unfulfilled dreams and passions.

Aren't you excited reading about all the various possibilities that will be available to you once your debt is eliminated? By creating a budget, setting financial goals, and having the determination to stick to your plans of action, you will be able you to enjoy the possibilities your money can offer you. Do you want to "just be paying off debt" the rest of your life? Think of all the compounding interest that is building up each month on every debt you owe which inevitably adds more debt to your already existing debt. What a limited and depressing future you will have! Take charge of your finances today so you can enjoy financial independence tomorrow.

David and I began our journey towards financial independence by creating our budget and then setting financial goals. We set short-term, mid-term and long-term financial goals for our family. The short-term goal was to control our day-to-day finances in order to track our spending to see where we could find some extra cash which we would allocate for our debt. Our mid-term goal was to begin making larger payments (rather than just the minimum payment) on our credit cards and student loans in order to pay off the debt. Our long-term goal was to begin building a savings because we literally had absolutely no money saved. We agreed to keep each other accountable for the goals we had set and also to stick to the budget we had created. We were committed to becoming debt free!

Chapter Nine

Drastic Changes

After David and I analyzed our budget and set financial goals, we also talked about our options regarding our financial predicament. After a couple of months of attempting to budget, we realized that our best intentions at resolving our financial predicament seemed futile because we were not making any progress. We knew that our debt was consuming us from every angle. We desperately wanted to eradicate our debt and no longer be tied down to it. David and I realized that we had two options—either meet with a financial counselor in order to get on a more solid repayment plan (three to five years) or sell our house in order to pay off the debt all at once. These were two of the most difficult decisions we have had to make. On the one hand, a financial counselor can get us out of debt, but it would take a few years. However, if we sold our house we could eliminate all of our debt immediately, but then we would have to uproot our family. We felt so torn between these two choices. Another thing that was important to us was for me to spend more time with our daughters. We wanted to create a plan that would enable us to reach our financial goals of becoming debt free and also allow me to spend more time with our children. We both knew that we needed to make some drastic changes to our lifestyle.

The choices and decisions we were in the process of making were met with apprehension from our friends and family. Questions such as, "Are you really sure you want to do this?" or "I do not think that is such a good idea." These types of inquiries made us at times doubt our decisions, but we decided to stick to the game plan we had chosen for our family. David and I had decided to sell our house. We agreed that this drastic change would be a sound financial decision since we could get double the amount we paid for it. We would use a portion of the net proceeds to pay off ALL of our outstanding debts. The remaining profit we would use as a down payment on another house. David and I had decided to purchase another house in the valley. Our house went on the market at the end of April 2005. We received several offers the weekend we listed the property. By Sunday evening, we looked over all the offers and submitted a counter offer to all the prospective buyers. Three days later we accepted an offer. We closed escrow at the end of May 2005. However, we did a lease-back on our house since our new house would not be ready until the middle of June. Since our house sold fairly quickly, we began to pack immediately after we accepted the offer on our house.

The reason we had purchased our new house in the valley was because it would leave us with only $103,000 mortgage. We wanted to have a more manageable mortgage to deal with and also with no other debt attached. Our mortgage on the house we sold was $325,000. Basically, my income was allocated to pay the mortgage. Therefore, our mortgage was taking half of our income every month. No wonder we were struggling to make ends meet. Experts advice homeowners to ensure that their mortgage payment be no more than a one-third of a family's income. We had far exceeded this amount! By analyzing our current debt-to-income ratio, we decided that another living arrangement needed to take place in order for us to begin the journey towards debt free living.

My family and I moved into our new home in the middle of June 2005. It was a hot and humid day to be moving in the valley. The temperature was probably around 100 degrees with extreme humidity. The weather was hot and sticky! With the help of our family and friends, we made it through that day and began settling into our new home. We were living on one income (David's) and we were comfortable financially. We were definitely not rich all of a sudden, but we were able to pay for our mortgage and basic necessities. I also did not work during that summer since I had resigned from the school district I had been employed at for the past seven years. The commute would have been too long (approximately one-and-a-half hours each way, if traffic was good). Therefore, I was able to stay home for that summer with our daughters.

Summer of 2005 was a very hot summer, but we attempted to adjust to the valley temperatures. Our daughters would go outside the house for approximately one or two hours a day. These hours were basically spent swimming in the association pool or going to the grocery store with me. It was extremely scorching hot to go outside to play! This weather was definitely tough on all of us, especially our girls because they were so used to going outside and playing in the backyard or at the park. We weren't able to do any of these things outside. We felt pretty confined to the house. Of course, I would try to take the girls to the mall or the grocery store just to get out of the house, but you can only do so many of these outings per week. Needless to say, we hated life in the valley. We felt isolated from the outside world. We missed our family and friends and the luxury of being able to go outdoors during the day. David and I were beginning to question whether or not we made the right decision in moving way out there. Even though we only lived about one hour away from our family and friends, it felt like we were living several states apart. We lived in the valley for eight weeks when we decided to move again.

We again sat down and looked at our budget to decide what our options were at this point. We knew that we wanted to move to an area that was more suitable weather wise and we definitely wanted to stay within our budget for housing needs. We finally decided to move into Orange County since this is where David's job is located. David had been commuting to work for about seven years. David was spending at the very least two hours a day commuting. He wanted to explore his options of whether he could move closer to his work. Buying a house was definitely out of the question for us. Orange County was at its peak with home sale prices and we definitely could not afford to purchase a house. We finally agreed that the only option for us was to find a house to rent in Orange County. We knew that our accountant would not be happy to hear that we would be renting rather than owning. Our accountant informed us of the tax incentives we get by owning a home. We told him that we knew about these incentives, but we just did not want to jeopardize our family's financial future. He understood even though he did not agree with our decision. Our accountant wanted to make sure that we fully understood the financial ramifications involved in selling our house.

In the middle of August 2005 we again, within a two-month period, put our house on the market. It sold the first weekend we listed the property. As soon as escrow opened on the house, we began searching for a rental property in Orange County. We found a house that met our standard of living, but more importantly, it was within our financial budget. In August, we began the moving process all over again. However, in the two months we had lived in the valley, I had managed to unpack our entire house. Once the house was completely unpacked, I threw away all the boxes and packing equipment we had used to pack our almost nineteen-hundred square foot house. Every single room in our house was completely furnished and then some. I have heard it said before that "you never know how much junk you accumulate over the years until you have to pack it all up!" How true this was for us! We definitely had way too much "junk" collected in our house. Now I had to start packing everything back up once again. I was overwhelmed to say the least! Nevertheless, I began the painstakingly difficult process to repack every nook and cranny of the now almost two-thousand-square-foot house.

Some people might look upon our experience as one of failure. But we choose to look upon it as a learning experience. David and I had never lived in the valley before, and now we know that this is not a place we will ever call home again. It sure was a hard way for us to learn this, but now we know. We will not let history repeat itself in this manner again! Another benefit we gained from selling our second house that same year was that we did not lose any money in the transaction of selling this second property. We actually profited approximately $25,000! It is not a lot of money, but to us the small profit was better than losing money.

Summer of 2005 was an extensive journey for us to travel through, but we believe that God was glorified in our effort to be committed to his principles of living a debt free life. All of our financial debts were paid in full. What a blessing and a relief this was for us! We were finally debt free! David and I had lived the last eight years under so much financial pressure to make ends meet. This burden of debt had at times threatened to end our marriage. Thank God that we made a commitment before him and our families that said we would stay together "in sickness and in health till death do us part"! Our marriage vows were and still are sacred vows we pledged to each other and to God. By God's grace we paid back every penny we had borrowed! We are no longer chained to our creditors, but freely and wisely living the life God intended for us to live. As I am writing this segment, I shed tears of joy at our accomplishment. By God's grace we are a testimony of His provision for our every need! We now prayerfully consider all financial transactions to ensure our debt free lifestyle! Every day for us is a choice to live debt free by making wise financial decisions in all of our financial transactions.

We have been renting for the last three years and we hope to purchase a house in the next couple of years. David decided to take all of our net proceeds from the sale of our two homes and place the money in several safe CD accounts. The interest we receive from our CDs pays for half our rent. We are now living a more peaceful life without the debt and creditors "knocking on our door." We are no longer in the rat race to keep our head above the water so as not to drown in our debt. David and I are still constantly bombarded by media advertisements to buy this and that, but we make choices every day about staying debt free. Now we are in a position of control over our finances and we decide what we "need" and what we "want". We are no longer letting ourselves be influenced by the media, but rather we are choosing what we will spend our money on. What a feeling of freedom we have! David and I know that renting is a temporary solution for us. We will eventually purchase a house of our own when we objectively decide that our mortgage payment will not jeopardize our family's financial situation. Our family has made many sacrifices over the last three years in order to become debt free and live within our means. It was a hard pill for us to swallow the notion of renting versus owning our own home, but we know that our family's financial future has a chance to flourish and thrive because of our frugal choices today.

Chapter Ten

Gluttony

The word frugal seems almost non-existent in the American vocabulary today. Our society has swung from one extreme to the other. When our parents were going through the Great Depression, frugality became the way of life for people. Our parents did without many of the luxuries we experience. However, today we have swung to the other side of the pendulum, and overindulgence never seems to satisfy our needs. We thirst for more and yet "more" never quenches our desire. We, as Americans, have become immune to the overindulgent nature we have created to the point of experiencing gluttony in our society today.

What is gluttony, you ask? Gluttony is the overindulgence and overconsumption of food, drink or materialism to the point of waste. Why is it that in our society today we experience such gluttony for foods and material possessions? We are in constant pursuit of better tasting foods and newer possessions. Americans never seem to be satisfied with the status quo of their lives. At what point have we crossed the line from being people who have simply reached for another glazed doughnut to being the global economy that prods its citizens to always buy more? Where have we crossed the line to become a people who individually and collectively are guilty of something that can be categorized as a sin?

In the Christian religion, gluttony is considered one of the seven deadly sins. What are the seven deadly sins, you ask? They are lust, pride, gluttony, envy, sloth, greed and anger. Gluttony seems to be as relevant a problem today as the rest of the seven deadly sins. Gluttony is viewed as a sin because we tend to focus on possessions obsessively to the point of saying that those items are the most important things in the world to us. This train of thought directly affects our relationship with God because we are creating a false god with the material possessions, food or drink which we have placed high on a pedestal. How, as a society, have we let this overindulgence with worldly things consume us to the point of being gluttonous? Do we not know when enough is enough?

Now let's take a look at your life. What have you experienced overindulgence with? Is it owning thirty pairs of shoes; consuming a whole pizza or a box of doughnuts on a regular basis; or purchasing clothes weekly even though you have brand new items in your closet with their price tags still attached? We cannot seem to get enough of trendy new restaurants, clothes, shoes, handbags, et cetera. So how do you know if you have crossed the line into gluttony? I believe that God gave each one of us an innate sense of what "enough" is. There is an inner guidance system within each of us that is infallible at deciphering when we have reached the point of full capacity. But why can't we ever hear this small but audible voice telling us when enough is enough? That is because we have become so preoccupied with what the media tells us that we forget to take time out and reflect upon what our inner selves are telling us. We, as a nation, are greatly influenced by the constant bombarding messages of the media advertisements.

The problem with media today is that we, as a society, have allowed it to become the center of what dictates our lives. The media greatly influences the public's decisions on what they will eat, drink, purchase, whether to engage in certain activities, trendy sayings, et cetera. The media uses this influence to market their products of choice without thinking of the negative ramifications this may cause the intended audience. We as consumers need to be proactive and find the faulty logic in the commercials and magazine advertisements so that we do not fall prey to their deceptive advertising. We need to ask ourselves if we really think that having the latest gadget or clothing will make us happier or more popular among friends. We as consumers need to realize that material possessions do not equal happiness. Rewarding ourselves with quality time with loved ones or diving into a favorite passion provides us with true happiness. Material objects are just a façade for happiness, and therefore we must use self-control in order to avoid our ravenous and gluttonous appetite for materialism.

As a society we often think of gluttony with a touch of irony. The irony of gluttony is that we imagine at first that we are grabbing all the happiness we can grab in its many varied forms. But the truth is that we are pushing it away from us. For example, let's use food as a representation of gluttony. It is not about enjoying the food, but rather it is about using it as an anesthetic. The first few bites of ice cream taste so good, but then we ingest the half-gallon of ice-cream in one sitting. After the first few bites we don't even taste the ice cream anymore. Gluttony, therefore, dulls the senses.

In *Willy Wonka and the Chocolate Factory,* Agustus Gloop is a perfect example of how gluttony manifests itself. Agustus consumes all the chocolate he can get his hands on with no end of ever being satisfied. What about our society's obsession with clothes? Our gluttonous nature has driven us to buy more and more clothing even though there are numerous outfits with price tags still attached in our closets. We simply are not satisfied! It seems that the more we consume, the bigger the void within us gets. Gluttony, therefore, from food or material possessions, never results in long-term happiness.

Gluttony is not necessary, despite popular belief, for us to experience happiness in our lives. The road to happiness is to do everything in moderation. Moderation is defined in the Webster's dictionary as "the capacity to exercise self-control; to limit oneself from overindulgence for the purpose of short-lasting pleasure; and allowing room for more enduring long-term happiness." Therefore, doing something "in moderation" means not doing it excessively. For instance, someone who moderates his food consumption eats when he is hungry and stops eating when his body communicates to him that hunger has been satisfied. Aristotle, the Greek philosopher, believed that moderation was the secret to a rich and content life. Besides Aristotle, the Bible also addresses the importance of moderation in our lives. The Biblical teachings of moderation (Ecclesiastes 7:18) and self-control (Galatians 5:23) are described in these verses. We are told that being extreme in either direction is not good for us and that we must exercise self-control over ourselves. "Do not join those who drink too much wine/ or gorge themselves on meat,/for drunkards and gluttons become poor,/ and drowsiness clothes them in rags" (Proverbs 23:20-21). This verse also implies that if you use food or drink in such a way as to injure your health or impair your mental capacity, then you are guilty of gluttony. It is clear from these three verses that if we do not practice moderation with all things, then gluttony becomes a very unwholesome state which leads to physical and/or mental suffering.

Gluttony, unfortunately, has become an epidemic in our society today. If you have read the mainstream media within the past year, then you know that too much gluttony is killing many of us right now. We are bombarded daily with ads for bacon cheeseburgers, soda and beer. On the other hand, we are obsessed with losing weight and getting buff. Gluttony is basically all about the "excess" in our lives. This excess refers to clothes, money, food, cars, boats, furniture, junk we collect, et cetera. As a nation, we have found countless ways to live out of proportion with the excess in our lives. But we choose not to see the physical and/or mental suffering we experience as a result of our excess. We are more comfortable seeing overeating as an addiction; excessive shopping as a weakness; and spending beyond our means as just a credit-rating problem. We are in denial as a nation, and unfortunately we are comfortable in this state of mind. Our gluttonous ways have forced us to recognize each other by our drive to consume. Whether this consumption is food or material possessions, it is evident by the lifestyle we lead. We need to change our attitudes about how much we consume and begin to live a lifestyle of moderation. Practicing moderation in all things keeps us from swinging to the extreme on either side of the pendulum.

Moderation in all things was the advice given to us by God in the Bible. Nothing is to be done in excess. For some reason in today's society it seems that enough is never enough. Gluttony has, obviously, taken over our lives to the point of not being able to exercise moderation and self-control. We seem to have failed as a nation to distinguish between what our needs and our wants really are. Instead of continuing the cycle of gluttony, let's sit down and reflect upon what are needs really are and what we view as wants in our lives.

Chapter Eleven

Needs vs. Wants

There are a few essential things which we need to survive, but there are multiple of wants we desire. A need is something you and I have to have and we cannot live without it. An example of this is food. If we do not eat, we will not survive for long. Therefore, our needs encompass such things as food to eat; a roof over our heads; a retirement savings when we age and monetary funds in order to purchase these basic needs. A want is something you and I would like to have, but this want is not absolutely necessary to sustain life. I wonder if in America, the land of prosperity, we really know the difference between a need and a want.

The world tells us that we do not have enough of this or we need that new and improved product in order to feel loved and accepted by others. So many of us buy into this lie and succumb to this lifestyle of needing this and that. Once we convince ourselves that we "have to have" that item, then we will stop at nothing to purchase this toy, whether or not we need it. The "it" becomes a need rather than a want. Therefore, we do not analyze whether or not we can afford this item. We purchase the "it" with one of two ways. We either pay cash or we charge it and worry about paying it off later. Most people do not have the cash upfront so they charge it. However, when later comes, we realize the funds originally allocated to pay off the item have been used to pay off other things which we purchased on yet another credit card. Therefore, the cycle of debt continues with no end in sight. We often wonder why we fret and agonize over our financial predicament as we lay our heads down at night to sleep; wake up in the middle of the night in a cold sweat; and wake up in the morning to an ominous gloom that has already taken over our day with financial uncertainty.

"Sale! Sale! Sale! Come one, come all!" Who hasn't heard the chant of every local retailer calling consumers to purchase the bargain of the century? Most of us know this calling as the one "we cannot afford to miss." However, if we are honest with ourselves, the sale actually becomes "the sale we cannot afford to own." As a society, we seem to overextend ourselves by purchasing one more of this or one more of that without giving much thought to the consequences of adding one more purchase to our already burden of credit card debit.

Where did we learn the art of managing our money? Most of us watched our parents wreak havoc with their financial situations and therefore became our models for managing our finances. Others were never taught how to balance a checkbook, and therefore they also end up in a vicious cycle of debt like their parents.

Staying out of debt is a choice. I personally make this choice on a daily basis. In order to help me make this choice, I choose to carry cash most of the time because this gives me a sense of exactly how much I am forking out of my wallet. For example, if I want to buy a sweater that costs $40, I will painstakingly take the cash out of my wallet and count every dollar in my possession to determine if this is indeed a wise purchase (a need) based on my financial allocation I have set aside for clothing for that particular month. If I feel that this sweater (a want) is costing me too much out of the clothing budget I have set for the month, then I will not be so tempted to make the purchase. However, if I just take out my debit card and hand it to the cashier, I will not give another thought as to how much I spent or if I could afford it. I have to keep track of my spending in order for me to visually see what my needs are and what my wants are. At times, I have noticed that my needs and wants sometimes get reversed since "I have to have" this or that. Unfortunately, I still get sucked in by the media advertisements which influence my financial choices. Therefore, I keep a list of the items I have purchased on a monthly basis in order for me to track my spending habits and assess whether some of the items purchased are really needs which I originally allocated money for. This simple worksheet gives me the incentive and motivation to review and make the necessary adjustments to my spending.

Take a moment to analyze your personal needs and wants. Your needs are the items necessary for your survival. Your wants are items you have purchased out of desire. Calculate the total monthly cost of your needs such as housing, food, utilities, clothing (just the basics), et cetera. What is the total monthly cost of your wants or items for which you may be making payments on that were purchased to satisfy your wants. These wants could be designer jeans, a watch, stereo system, et cetera. Are you spending as much for your needs as you are for your wants? Try to identify ways in which you can cut corners in the future to save more money.

Needs vs Wants Worksheet

Needs (Necessary for survival)	Cost	Wants (Purchased out of desire)	Cost
Total cost of needs		Total cost of wants	

Once you have established what your needs and wants are, then you can take the time and explore alternative ways in which you can still enjoy your wants. The alternative methods consist of paying less for what you want. There are many opportunities for you and me to seek out our wants, but for a fraction of the cost. For example, I love to read! I love to read fiction novels, biographies, autobiographies, et cetera. The library would be one way for me to fulfill part of this hobby, but I want to keep the books I read. The library obviously requires that I return the books I borrow. The bookstore is another place for me to get books, but for a hardcover book I could be paying anywhere from $20 to $25 for just one book. So I am left in a predicament. I cannot keep the library books and I cannot afford to buy a new book every time I finish the one I am reading. This is an expensive WANT for me, so I have found an alternative method of fulfilling my WANT. My local library has a small bookstore where individuals in my community can drop off their unwanted books. The selection at this little bookstore is incredible and the price for these books is unbelievably affordable. I can get a hardcover book for $1, $2 or $3 per book. I have not paid over $3 for a book since I have been utilizing this bookstore for my love of reading. Most of the books are fairly new releases and choices I have been meaning to read but could not afford the bookstore prices. I love to read the Oprah Book Club choices, the John Grisham novels and also the Christian books that are also available at this little bookstore. The drawback to utilizing this bookstore is that I cannot get the "just released" copy of a particular book. But to me, when I do find that book several months later, it is well worth the wait at the price I am paying for that particular book. Delayed gratification does have its rewards! This is just one method of satisfying a want that fits within my budget.

As you can see, sticking to a budget does not mean that you have to give up all of your wants. There are numerous discount and low-cost methods of attaining your wants. You have to investigate and explore your community and your resources around you in order to find alternative methods to fulfill your wants and desires.

Chapter Twelve

Bargain Shopping

As discussed, there are numerous alternative methods of saving money. Most people know about the traditional methods of saving money such as clipping coupons or shopping the sales at the mall. However, be creative in your search for additional methods that may exist in your community. If you are unsure of where to start your search, begin by asking some of your friends what they do to cut costs and save money. You would be surprised at what you hear!

One of my friends loves to shop the local bakery outlet for bread, cookies, cakes, et cetera. She says that she usually pays half the cost (or even less sometimes) than the grocery store charges on many items. I asked her what the quality of the products is like and she said that her family cannot tell the difference between the grocery store-bought items and the outlet bakery products. I have tried this method of saving money and it was great! I paid less for the items purchased and my family enjoyed the mouthwatering desserts and pastries. What a great cost-effective idea!

Like my friend, I also love to bargain shop! Whenever I find a great deal, I feel ecstatic because I took the time to look at other options before going to the mall and just paying for that particular item at full price. When my kids were infants and toddlers, I was fortune to have several consignment stores nearby where I could shop for items they needed. I usually paid half the price (less than half at times) of an item's full retail price. I would find great deals on clothes, shoes and bedding and even on luxuries such as toys. The kids enjoyed their "new" clothes or toys without giving it a second thought of where the item was purchased. I, of course, relished in the fact that I received such a bargain.

Now that my kids are older I still choose to shop at the local Goodwill store. There are so many great items that are donated by others and for a fraction of the cost originally paid for those items. When I found out I was pregnant with our third child, I realized that I had given away all of my baby furniture and clothes. I knew that I did not want to purchase brand new items such as a crib, high chair, stroller, et cetera. These types of baby items are extremely expensive when you have to purchase all of these necessities yourself, which is what I was faced with. I decided to keep my eye out for any items I might come across while shopping at Goodwill. What a blessing! One day I found a beautiful white crib for $25. My family and friends could not believe that I purchased something so nice from the thrift store. It looked brand new! On another day I found a good quality high chair for $9.99. What a bargain! There were other items I found such as a brand new (I could not tell that it had been used) Peg-Perego car seat (with base) for $9.99; an extra saucer for $5.99; et cetera. Besides purchasing baby items, I have also bought clothing such as jackets, pants, shirts, et cetera for the kids. Of course, you have to be selective about the clothes you find at the thrift store. Some of the clothing has stains and tears that are not fixable. You as the consumer have to examine every article that you are interested in purchasing so that you are not surprised when you get home and find an untreatable stain or tear. There is a no return policy once an item has been purchased at the thrift store so you need to ensure that you indeed are getting a great deal for your money. With this being said, I have to tell you that I have found clothing in great condition that I have purchased for the kids with brand names such as Gap, Limited Too, ROXY, Gymboree, Abercrombie & Fitch, Disney Store, et cetera. When my kids wear their clothing, people always marvel at how beautifully my daughters are dressed. Therefore, whether I am shopping at the mall (which I do from time to time) or at the thrift store, I take pride in dressing my kids. There are many additional items to be found at my local thrift store that I have also purchased such as kitchen supplies, electrical appliances, furniture, et cetera for incredible prices. Not only do I benefit from great bargains at the Goodwill store, but when I make a purchase others benefit as well. By shopping a Goodwill thrift store, I am helping to fund training programs for individuals with physical and mental disabilities and other barriers to independence they may be facing. I am helping my community out by providing individuals with disabilities with vocational training and jobs. Everyone benefits by shopping at the neighborhood Goodwill store!

By now, you get my drift. My point is that you can find great deals on products you need and even want, but you have to employ delayed gratification. What I mean is that you have to be willing to wait long enough for a product to become available at a discounted price rather than paying "an arm and a leg" for it. There is no shame in getting a used item for less. However, it is a shame when you come to the end of the month and you do not have enough money to pay your bills or buy groceries because you already spent the money on that brand new item you just could not wait to get your hands on. I have learned many times about my shame and guilt in not having enough money at the end of the month to pay my bills or buy groceries because I had already spent the allocated funds on other brand new items.

When it is all said and done, keep in mind that most people do not even know where you purchased an item unless you tell them. Therefore, if you have any qualms about telling others where you shop for your things, then make it a habit not to disclose this information. For example, no one has to know where you shop for your kids' clothing. One of my pastor's once said, "No child cares what brand name clothing they are wearing as long as they feel loved and respected by their family." How true that is! We as parents seem to be the only ones obsessed with which brand name clothing we dress our kids in. Whom are we trying to impress anyway—our kids' friends or our adult friends? I think we all know the answer to this (our adult friends, of course). Therefore, if you feel embarrassed about telling others that you shop at the Goodwill store for your kids, then feel free to omit this information from your conversation with others. This will be your little secret that is enabling your family to survive financially in a world where most people are living beyond their financial means. No one has to know the length you are going to in order to ensure your families financial stability.

What if you and I were having a conversation and you told me that there is no way that you would ever wear clothing worn by another person? However, you are looking to minimize your clothing budget and you would like to know whether there are other alternatives besides shopping the big expensive malls for the brand name clothing you want to wear. Let's face it, even the sales at the mall are not always good bargains. My next question to you would be, "Have you ever heard of ROSS, Marshalls, TJ Max, et cetera?" These stores are constantly advertising that they can save you between forty percent and sixty percent off department store prices on brand name items. Why not save a buck, as the expression goes. I have been able to find items from shoes to clothing to handbags from designer names such as Tommy Hilfiger, Nine West, Ralph Lauren, et cetera for a fraction of the price. If I can get the same sweater at these stores for less than the department stores are advertising the item for, why wouldn't I purchase it? I choose to save a buck and not shop department store prices. How about you? How much money are you spending on brand name clothing at the mall? More importantly, how much money can you be saving from shopping at these discount retail stores? Track your monthly spending on your clothing allowance and compare prices.

What about big expensive furniture to furnish your home? A friend of mine told me of another alternative avenue where you can save money. If you are in need of furniture for your home, then she says that you have to check out the various consignment stores first before you go out and pay full price to furnish your home. Of course, make sure that you do your homework beforehand and research prices at the retail stores in order to compare the prices at the consignment stores. You want to make sure that you are indeed getting a good deal on the gently used furniture. My friend purchased a couple of pieces of furniture from a consignment store and she loves the "new" additions to her home. If she hadn't told me, I would never have known that those items were "gently used" pieces of furniture, because they looked brand new to me. Furniture could be quite costly, but if you shop around you would be surprised at the bargains you will find! Make sure to also check out the furniture deals available on websites such as craigslist.org and eBay. The possibilities are endless! You will be able to furnish your home for pennies on the dollar.

If you are the type of person who truly refuses to purchase used furniture, but you still want to get a great bargain, then there are other stores where you can purchase furniture for a fraction of the cost. Have you heard of Costco, Sam's Club, department store outlets, et cetera? These warehouse stores from time to time get beautiful brand new furniture at a bargain of a price. To give you an example, David and I wanted to buy some nice new living room furniture. The furniture that existed in our living room at that time was old college furniture we both had accumulated while attending Long Beach State. The furniture was old, dirty and probably had been handed down to us from several roommates over the years. Neither one of us could remember exactly how we had stumbled across the college furniture. That should give you an idea of how old our college furniture really was. The "catch" to our situation, however, was that we only had $1000 to spend. We obviously knew that a $1000 would not get us very far if we went to a department store to purchase our furniture. We both kept our eyes open to find a great bargain. One day while we were shopping for our groceries at Costco, we came across a Bassett couch and loveseat set we both really liked. We checked out the price and realized that we could also afford to buy a new coffee table to go with our new set of couches. For these three brand new items we paid (taxes included) $998. What a bargain! We were so ecstatic that when we came home, we told our families, and they were shocked that we were able to get so many new pieces of furniture for so little money. The next day when our families came over, they marveled at the beautiful furniture. All I can say is that there is a reward in persevering! Shop around and compare prices, because your wallet will thank you!

Another place where we were able to get some nice pieces of brand new furniture for our home was at a Wickes furniture outlet. This warehouse has a great deal of new furniture that has either been discontinued or slightly damaged that Wickes is selling for a bargain of a price. The furniture outlet carries items from bedroom sets to dining room tables. There is a great selection of items to pick from depending on what you are looking for. For example, David and I needed a dresser with a mirror that would match our dark cherry bedroom set. We were very excited when we found our brand new dark cherry dresser for only $199 and the matching mirror for only $50. The entire dresser with mirror was $249. What a bargain! We were able to save money and also gain some nice new pieces of furniture for our home by shopping at the warehouse prices.

By being frugal in your spending, you are not only saving money, but you are also inadvertently helping to improve your credit score. All the money you are saving could potentially be paying off your debt which in effect improves your credit score. So as the saying goes, you are killing two birds with one stone. Who could not use a boost to their credit score?

Chapter Thirteen

What Is Your Credit Score?

Experts agree that a person's credit score is really the key to his/her financial life. Credit scores are used by a number of people and businesses including mortgage lenders, employers, insurance agents, landlords, credit card companies, et cetera, which inevitably determine the fate of a person's ability to acquire these venues. It is extremely important for you to maintain your creditworthiness, because these people and businesses ultimately determine the quality of our lives. What I mean by this is that these institutions have the power to raise or lower the interest rate on a loan (car, mortgage, credit card, etc.) or whether or not you acquire that apartment or house you want to rent. So what exactly is a credit score, you ask? A credit score is a number that reflects how likely you are to repay your debts. Your credit score basically tells a lender very quickly and efficiently how likely you are to either repay or default on a loan. Therefore, the lower the credit score, the higher the interest rate you will have to pay because the lender has to take on more risk to lend you money based on your past credit history. On the other hand, the higher your credit score is the lower your interest rate will be. The best way to attain a good credit score is to establish credit by having a few credit cards and loans, paying your bills on time and keeping your debts at a minimum.

There are several scoring methods to attain your credit score, but the most common is the FICO score. FICO was developed by the Fair Isaac Corporation which is a leading credit analysis and risk management firm. You can access your FICO score by logging onto www.myfico.com. FICO scores can range from 300 to 850. A score of 720 and higher indicates a good credit rating and anything below 600 is considered not so good credit. Get to know your credit score!

Now that you know the importance of knowing your credit score, do you know what your actual credit score is? David and I have made it a priority to know what our individual credit scores are. David has a score of 815 and I have a score of 750. I have to tell you that I was a little disappointed that my credit score was not as high as David's, but I also know why. I have mentioned earlier that I had a habit of regularly opening up credit card accounts, and this inadvertently hurt my credit score. You can have three or four credit card accounts open without negatively impacting your credit score, but I had over nine credit cards open at any given time. You can say that I "charged" my way into debt. My credit score was further affected when I decided to close all of my credit card accounts, except for one, after we paid off all of our outstanding debts. I now know that closing credit card accounts also negatively impacts my credit score. I have learned the hard way the importance of keeping up a high credit score.

Now that you are clear about what a credit score is, do you know what a credit report is? Many people today are confused about the difference between a credit score and a credit report. There is a common misconception that a credit score is the same as a credit report and vice versa. This is not accurate information. Your credit report is a listing of your credit activity which is provided by one or all of the three major credit reporting agencies. These agencies are Experian, TransUnion, and Equifax. Typically, your credit report consists of items such as closed and open credit accounts, account balances, payment delinquencies and any inquiries made into your credit file. Your credit score is also called "credit rating." This credit score is a rating based on the information found in your credit report. Your credit score is a numerical comparison to other people's scores which then may be used by banks, mortgage lenders and loan companies, et cetera to determine your creditworthiness. The higher your credit score is the better your chances are for acquiring incentives from banks and other lending institutions. Lending institutions that use credit scores to rate creditworthiness will tend to offer credit to those people with higher scores. Of course, there are other factors that these institutions consider when they are providing loans to you and me. Some of these factors are length of employment, current income, current debt, et cetera. Therefore, your credit score (which is crucial) is not the only determining factor in acquiring a loan.

There are a variety of factors, negative and positive, that can affect your credit score. These four factors include credit usage, credit accounts, payment history, and length of credit history. Here is a numerical breakdown of how your credit score is calculated: 35 percent payment history; 30 percent outstanding debt; 15 percent length of your credit history; 10 percent recent inquiries on your credit report; and 10 percent types of credit in use. These percentages outline the weight placed on each of the above factors when calculating your credit score. Notice the importance of paying your past debts and eliminating present debt.

The first factor in calculating your credit score is credit usage which is based on the ratio of debt versus income. High balances (debt) generally have a negative impact on your credit score. Lenders evaluate how much you owe in relation to how much you own and also in relation to how much you earn (income) in order to help them determine your creditworthiness. They might look at your score and wonder if your debt to income ratio will allow you to repay the loan. On the other hand, low balances are typically a positive factor. However, if your balances are low because you do not use your credit accounts, lenders do not have the information to determine how you pay your debts. Many people would rather have this type of dilemma rather than too much debt. No matter which side of the spectrum you are on, your credit score is a balancing act that can mean the difference between an excellent score and one that needs improving.

The second factor is credit accounts. How many open installment loans (not including your mortgage) do you have? When you have accounts listed in your credit report, lenders can view your payment history. This can be a positive step in your favor if your payment history is good. However, having too many accounts open may be a negative because lenders may be concerned that you are spending (or preparing to spend) beyond your means.

The third factor is payment history. In a nutshell, the better your payment history, the higher your credit score. Any missed payments will negatively affect your score. Missing one single payment, however, may not be as harmful as missing several consecutive payments. Many lenders consider missing three or more consecutive payments as an indication that they may never be repaid.

The fourth factor is your length of credit history. How long have you had your credit accounts? Usually, the longer you have had your accounts open, the easier it is for lenders to evaluate how you typically use your credit and repay your debts. Therefore, the longer your accounts have been open and the better your payment history, the more positive your credit rating will be.

If you have less than perfect credit, then you should consider some of these tactics that will help raise your credit score. Here are some tips for raising your credit score: paying all your monthly debts on time; keeping your debt level down; paying your credit card balances on time so you do not incur late and over the limit fees; do not apply for a lot of credit accounts; do not close long-standing accounts; and correct any problems or mistakes in your credit history. If you employ these strategies than your credit score will rise to a level that represents your creditworthiness.

Did you know that the average United States credit score is 675? (www-credit-score.info). Have you checked your credit score lately? Under a new federal law, you have the right to receive a free copy of your credit report once every twelve months from each of the three nationwide consumer reporting agencies (Experian, Equifax, and Trans Union). To request your free annual report under this law, go to www.annualcreditreport.com. This websites offers you an opportunity to freely access your credit report. Take advantage of it!

In recent years, there has been a dramatic increase in identity theft crimes. This could potentially harm your credit. Identity theft crimes refer to different types of crime in which someone wrongfully obtains and uses your personal information in order to commit fraud for his/her own economic gain. Your personal information includes your Social Security number, bank account and credit card numbers, and other valuable identifying data that others could use to profit at your expense. It is possible that someone might have done something to your credit without your knowledge. If this activity negatively affected your credit report, then most likely it will have a harmful impact on your credit score. It is wise to attempt to resolve the debt as quickly as possible. There are also unintentional errors that are made to credit reports by lending institutions. These mistakes could force you to pay higher interest rates or even cause you to be turned down for a loan. You owe it to yourself to stay informed regarding the information found in your credit report.

Many people, unfortunately, have fallen prey to identity theft crimes. Some have reported that unauthorized individuals have taken funds out of their bank accounts, used their credit cards without their consent, and in the worst cases individuals have taken over their identities altogether in order to incur enormous debts and commit crimes while using the victim's name. In many cases, a victim's losses include not only financial losses, but also substantial additional financial costs that are associated with trying to restore his/her reputation and correcting the false information the criminal incurred. Due to victims being violated in such a manner, Congress was prompted in 1998 to create a new federal law that labels identity theft a crime in the United States. Individuals are now protected by this federal law, but it is still up to each of us to be proactive in maintaining good credit ratings. Here are some tips to be mindful of in order to protect yourself against identity theft: 1) Be careful about giving out your personal information to others unless you have initiated the transaction. 2) Remember to check your financial information (bank accounts, credit cards, etc. regularly. 3) Check your credit report at least once per year to ensure that no transactions have taken place without your knowledge (take advantage of your free credit report). It is important to be proactive in protecting your name and credit.

Did you know that even if you are diligent about checking your financial papers, identity theft could still happen to you? Statistics show that every three seconds someone becomes the victim of an identity theft crime. The only way for you to know whether or not someone is using your identity at your financial expense is after they have committed the crime in your name. What if you had the opportunity to stop a criminal from using your credit before a crime is actually committed? Would you take advantage of this opportunity? Well, now you can protect your credit by enrolling in LifeLock at www.lifelock.com or calling 1-877-LifeLock (1-877-543-3562). LifeLock offers a proven solution that prevents your identity from being stolen before it happens. Don't you want this type of protection for your financial assets you have worked so hard to achieve? LifeLock has been featured on MSNBC and the Today Show and it is endorsed by the Better Business Bureau (BBB). LifeLock costs just $10 per month to protect a lifetime of assets. As part of this enrollment fee, you receive fraud alerts that are established with the three major credit bureaus; a $1 million service guarantee; from now on every time you apply for a line of credit you will be contacted by phone to ensure that it is you applying for credit and not someone else; junk mail will be restricted (statistics show this is one of the most common ways thieves hijack your identity); pre-approved lines of credit blocked (all of those annoying pre-approved credit offers are gone); you will receive credit reports from the three major credit bureaus; fraud alerts are placed on file with the credit bureaus; and so many more benefits. You receive all of these services for just $10 a month. Wow, what a bargain! David and I thought so too. We enlisted with LifeLock to protect the good credit we have worked so hard to attain. David and I wanted to be responsible financial stewards of the finances with which we had been entrusted and not be violated by someone who wanted to ruin our good name and credit rating.

David and I fell victim to an identity theft crime before we enrolled with LifeLock. I requested a copy of my credit report while we were in the process of purchasing our house in the valley, and I was scanning my report to ensure that all of my outstanding debts had been paid. Suddenly, I noticed a loan of $2500 that was listed under a particular bank. I was perplexed by this amount because I couldn't remember ever taking out a loan for this amount from this particular bank. I called my husband, David, at work to inform him of this apparent transaction. Since this unknown debt was only showing on my credit report and not on his, I asked him if he ever remembered my taking out this loan. He stated that he had no recollection of my signing any loan documents for this amount of money. I immediately called the financing institution that was handling our mortgage transaction and informed them that I wanted to appeal the unknown debt on my credit report. They informed me that they would attempt to resolve the matter as soon as I put a written letter together stating my concern. I had to also list important numbers on this letter such as my phone number, address, Social Security number, the account number in question, et cetera. I earnestly drafted this dispute letter and faxed it to the mortgage representative. He called me later that day to inform me that he had received my letter and that he had sent it to the dispute center. He said that I should hear back in written form in about thirty days from the institution regarding the disputed debt. Sure enough, at the end of that month a letter came addressed to me stating that the debt had been fraudulent since that particular bank did not have any record of my signing any loan documents for the $2500. They also stated that they would eradicate this debt from my credit report. This letter also advised me to run another credit report in approximately six months to ensure that the $2500 debt had been removed from my file. I am so glad that I took the time to review the outstanding accounts on my credit report. After six months, I ran another report and this time there were no outstanding balances. The debt in question had been removed from my credit report. This is one of the many reasons why I must check my credit report on a consistent basis.

Did you know that the three major credit bureaus also sell your personal information to third party marketing companies? It's true! Have you ever noticed how after you apply for a mortgage or consumer credit cards, you begin to receive unsolicited inquiries for pre-approved credit cards or other related offers? The credit bureaus are selling your personal information! If you have LifeLock then your personal information is restricted from being sold. However, if you do not have LifeLock, then there are some things you can do. You can stop this potentially dangerous exchange of your personal information by using a simple opt-out feature.

You can contact the three major credit bureaus to opt-out so that your name, address and personal information is not compromised. Call (888) 567-8688 or log onto www.optoutprescreen.com to make your voice heard. Consumers can also contact each credit bureau individually:

- Consumer Opt-Out, Experian, 701; Experian Pkwy, Allen, TX 75013
- Options, Equifax, Inc. P.O. Box 740123, Atlanta, GA 30374 – 0123
- Name Removal Option, Trans Union Corp., P.O. Box 97328, Jackson, MS 39288

When opting out, consumers have two options. You will need to specify which option you are choosing. The two options are: 1) a five year opt-out (it stops them from selling your name for five years); and 2) a permanent opt-out (it permanently stops them from selling your name). Make your voice heard regarding your personal information! We have all heard the frightening statistics regarding identity theft. It is the country's fastest growing crime. We do not want to fall victim to such schemes! We must do everything within our power to protect ourselves and our financial resources we have worked so hard to attain.

Chapter Fourteen

Bankruptcy

David and I have made a personal commitment that no matter how much debt we have accumulated, we will never file for bankruptcy. We believe that bankruptcy has become a scapegoat for so many people to not be held responsible for repaying their debts. By God's grace, we will do everything in our power to repay our obligations to our debtors if we ever become engulfed in our debts again. God gave us the ability and the resources to repay our original debt of $55,000. If we ever do become trapped again (which I hope we do not) with a large sum of debt, my hope and prayer is that we do the right thing again by repaying our debtors rather than taking the easy way out and filing for bankruptcy. We believe bankruptcy should only be considered as a last resort for a couple of reasons. First and foremost, God requires each of us to repay our debts. We need to face our financial responsibilities rather than using bankruptcy as a means to avoid paying debts. Secondly, your credit will be blemished because a bankruptcy remains on a credit bureau report for ten years. Ten years is definitely a long time for a credit report to be labeled as once being delinquent. With these two reasons in mind, one has to ask why so many people are still filing for bankruptcy.

Did you know that in 2004, there were 1.6 million households (American Bankruptcy Institute) that filed for bankruptcy protection? This is an astronomical number when compared to thirty years ago when bankruptcy was almost non-existent. The majority of the 1.6 million households that declared bankruptcy was a direct result of the poor financial decisions people made. When those unsolicited pre-approved credit card offers came in the mail, many people felt compelled to use the available credit that was being extended to them without thinking of the negative ramifications. The availability of credit that was generously being extended was NOT a requirement to borrow money. Those people choose to borrow the money of their own free will.

During the last thirty years, society has witnessed an explosive growth in the number of consumer bankruptcies that are filed in the United States every year. American households need to accept personal responsibility for the debt incurred from borrowed money rather than declaring bankruptcy. Repaying debt is a responsibility or an oath you take and not a choice of "if" you are going to repay the borrowed money.

Bankruptcy was once regarded as a shameful and humiliating failure. The stigma associated with bankruptcy was often seen as a flaw in a person's character because of an inability to meet one's commitment to repay debt. However, in our society today, bankruptcy has become an everyday fact of life. There are millions of American consumers who are struggling with their record breaking debt. People with big debt loads often see their credit scores suffer, and frequently they make matters worse by falling behind on their payments as they attempt to juggle various bills. To compound their debt problems, lenders eventually raise the interest rates adding even more debt to the average American debt load. One has to step back and analyze what is really behind the bankruptcy boom. In simplest terms, it stems from a growing tendency for consumers to spend more than they can afford to repay. Our society has developed the mentality of "spend now and save later." This type of mentality, which has gripped the nation, has already led to a record number of people being plunged into bankruptcy.

The credit card companies have greatly influenced the "spend now and save later" culture of our society. Americans are constantly being tempted to borrow and spend with absolutely no thought to creating savings accounts and planning for their financial future. How could we think of our financial future when we are constantly being bombarded by the credit card companies? Americans receive numerous credit card offers daily in the mail enticing them to open accounts with zero percent interest or other short-term incentives that eventually fade after several months. Then the consumer feels trapped with the credit card balance and also with the rising interest rate that was not originally present when the account was first opened. Credit card companies surely know how to lure us in as consumers and then they have us trapped with our overwhelming debt.

Credit card companies have also become extremely creative in their means to create slogans to attract consumers into opening accounts. Americans have become so immune to the credit card slogans that we do not even give them a second thought as to what they really mean. Some credit card slogans state "charge it – the easy way to pay" or "life takes Visa." Are we really buying into these messages? Obviously, using a credit card is easier to use than writing a check, but this "ease" is only temporary. When the credit card statement comes, reality sets in and we realize that "charging it" was really not the easiest way to pay for those particular items. What about the Visa slogan? We have all seen the commercial where everyone is using a Visa card and everything is running smoothly, but when one person attempts to pay with cash then the whole world seems to halt at this "atrocity." We have to step back and analyze this commercial rather than become immune to its meaning. What is wrong with paying cash for your purchases rather than running up debt on your credit card? There is absolutely nothing wrong with paying cash, which is therefore allowing you to live within your means. The credit card companies want you to think otherwise because ultimately they are the ones who will benefit from your inability to pay off the credit card balance. Americans need to become more proactive in using their judgment in deciphering whether or not a credit card slogan or incentive should be taken at face value. We are constantly being inundated with advertisements which are directed at luring us into financial traps. The slogans and incentives offered by the credit card companies are apparently working because so many Americans are up to their eyeballs in debt. The ramifications of so many being enticed into these offers are that they are not able to repay their debt, which consequently leads to millions of Americans filing for bankruptcy.

There are two basic types of bankruptcy proceedings: Chapter 7 and Chapters 11, 12, and 13. The bankruptcy proceedings can either be chosen by the debtor or initiated by creditors. A filing under Chapter 7 is called liquidation or selling of assets. It is the most common type of bankruptcy proceeding. Liquidation involves the appointment of a trustee who collects the property of the debtor, sells it and distributes the funds to the creditors to pay off the exiting debt. Under Chapter 7 bankruptcy, a debtor is allowed to exempt certain property from being sold. The list of exempt property could include household furniture, jewelry, house, clothing, pensions, insurance policies, et cetera. However, each state is allowed to opt-out of the federal exemptions and provide their own list of items that could not be liquidated. Therefore, exemptions under Chapter 7 bankruptcy can vary widely from state to state. Bankruptcy proceedings under Chapters 11, 12, and 13 involve the rehabilitation of the debtor to allow him or her to use future earnings to pay off creditors. Basically, these types of bankruptcies allow the debtor to repay his creditors over a three- to five-year period with the income the debtor accumulates during this time. A trustee is appointed to receive payments from the debtor and then the trustee disburses the funds to the creditors. Unlike Chapter 7 bankruptcy, a debtor remains in possession of all his property.

In April 2005, Congress passed a reform to the Bankruptcy Prevention and Consumer Protection Act. This act resulted in major reforms in the bankruptcy law such as placing stricter guidelines on people filing for Chapter 7 bankruptcies. Many Chapter 7 bankruptcies are now looking more like Chapter 11 or 13 because debtors are forced to pay off their existing debt rather than liquidating their assets. Congress is forcing more people to take responsibility for their debt rather than dismissing or liquidating their assets. Other factors that came into this reform include audits, credit counseling prior to filing for bankruptcy, financial education before being dismissed from debt, et cetera. With these restrictions, it is important to know that a debtor is allowed to file for bankruptcy only once every six years. There are many adverse consequences to bankruptcy and a debtor must be wise when choosing this route.

Before you become another statistic in the bankruptcy arena, seek some counsel from professionals who are trained in alleviating debt. There are numerous credit counseling agencies around and these professionals will help you look at all your financial options such as debt consolidation, debt settlement or credit counseling programs. By working with a credit counseling agency and researching the various programs they offer, you will be able to lower your monthly payments (possibly up to 70 percent), drastically reduce your interest rates, (rates ranging between 6 percent and 8 percent) and even eliminate late fees and over the limit charges.

Anyone who has ever faced a financial crisis has fantasized about getting a fresh start. A credit counseling agency can give you that new beginning and a fresh start with your finances. Working with a credit counselor will give you an accountability partner as well as a trained financial expert who will assist you in devising a plan of attack that fits your personal financial budget. The credit counselor will customize your debt plan so that you will achieve success with your finances. Your debt plan may look something like this: 1) devise a battle plan; 2) go on a cash diet; 3) sell assets; 4) negotiate with your credit lenders; 5) look for alternative ways to bring in extra cash flow. These are just some of the items that might be listed on the budget plan you and your credit counselor draft up. Let's take a look at these five simple yet effective strategies that will enable you to pay off your debt and avoid bankruptcy.

1) Devise a battle plan. You and your credit counselor will be able to sit down and look at all your bills. First, the counselor will look at your secured debts such as your home and your car. How much are they costing you each month and what are the interest rates? Secondly, the counselor will examine the mandatory monthly bills such as your phone, power, groceries, insurance, et cetera. Third, the credit counselor will examine your unsecured debt such as your credit cards and evaluate your interest rates on these cards. Lastly, the counselor will look at the expendables such as cable, gym membership, eating out and other optional purchases. Now that you and your credit counselor have an idea of what your monthly expenses are, it is time to slice and dice. You will be going through each category and looking for ways to cut out excess expenses. You obviously need a roof over your head, electricity, food, water, transportation and health insurance. Everything else is negotiable. Pay for your basic necessities first each month and then evaluate the leftover income to decide which debts you will attack for that month.

2) Go on a cash diet. A cash diet allows you to go on an allowance system for yourself. From each paycheck, you will take out a set amount in cash. You and your credit counselor will determine in advance what will be a reasonable amount of cash for you to withdraw. This cash allowance you have predetermined has to last you either the entire month or till the next paycheck, whatever period of time you established with your credit counselor. Once the cash runs out, then you need to make do with what you already have in your possession till the next allowance period.

3) Sell assets. Do you have items you own that you could live without if you were to sell them? Anything that you think has cash value and you can part with, sell it! These items can include antiques, an old car, baseball collection, clothes, other collectibles, et cetera. Make sure that you check all areas such as the closets, garage, storage unit, et cetera. Any extra cash that you can bring in will therefore help you pay down your debt. Here are some ideas of how you can sell your items: eBay, garage sale, craigslist.org, consignment shops, et cetera. The possibilities are endless! Remember, one man's junk is another man's treasure.

4) Negotiate with your credit lenders. You and your credit counselor will begin the process of negotiating with your creditors by either lowering the interest rate, lowering the monthly payment or doing away with interest temporarily in order to give you enough time to get back on your feet financially. When creditors see that you are working with a credit counseling agency, oftentimes they are more willing to cut you a deal in the negotiation phase.

5) Look for alternative ways to bring in extra cash flow. Let's face it, between garage sales and eBay you can only make so much revenue. Have you ever thought about alternative and creative ways in which you can make a little more income with either a part-time job or a hobby? Some people choose to mow lawns or clean houses on the weekend for extra income. Others have a hobby or interest that they can market out to the world. Still others can use their Monday through Friday professions to get some consulting work on the side. For example, a friend of mine is a social worker during the week, and on the side she also does home studies for an adoption agency for extra income. Research and explore the possibilities in your community. There is no shame in working outside the Monday through Friday job in order to incur additional income revenue in order to pay down your debt and avoid bankruptcy.

Filing for bankruptcy is not the only option. There are alternative means by which debt can be repaid over time. The road to financial freedom involves making some tough decisions along the way. Therefore, building a solid financial future requires discretion in handling finances and saying "NO" to any unnecessary borrowing and spending. It is possible to get out of debt responsibly and efficiently. You have to have the determination and perseverance to repay those from whom you have borrowed.

If you have no other alternative and you do have to file for bankruptcy, then you need to know that bankruptcy comes at a cost both on a personal and financial level. On a personal level, it becomes fairly humiliating having to admit that you had to file bankruptcy since you were not responsible enough with your finances to repay the outstanding debts. On a financial level, there are many aspects of life which are adversely influenced by your decision to file for bankruptcy. One of these factors is having to pay a higher interest rate when purchasing a vehicle or acquiring credit cards. Depending on the lender, these interest rates can at times be double what they normally are! Other repercussions of bankruptcy are finding places to live and acquiring jobs. Many people who file for bankruptcy get turned down for apartments, home loans and jobs because of the blemished record that appears when these prospective agencies run a credit report. As you can see, there are numerous implications if you choose bankruptcy. However, if you acquire additional revenue, you can avoid bankruptcy, pay off debt and begin building your savings and retirement portfolios.

Chapter Fifteen

Retirement and Savings

A dramatic change is taking place across America. The country is realizing that traditional sources of retirement income from pension plans and Social Security are quickly diminishing. Retirees will soon be dependent on personal savings and part-time work for a majority of their income. Therefore, with longer life expectancies due to medical breakthroughs and rising costs due to inflation, it is critical that Americans understand the importance of saving today. This means that Americans must save an adequate amount of money prior to retirement and also make intelligent investment decisions with their savings. In a sense, the future of America rests on the ability of workers to save and invest properly. However, not enough people are saving for their retirement.

Are you contemplating saving for retirement? Are you sure that you will have all the money you will need to survive financially at retirement? If you are like many people today, the answer is probably no. If you have just begun your career, you are probably not thinking about your retirement, since you tell yourself that you will have plenty of time to plan and save at a later date. However, for some, retirement may just be a few years away, and they have not begun to invest for their retirement years. There is no time like the present to start planning for your future no matter where you find yourself on the retirement spectrum. Financial experts encourage you to start planning and saving early to have the financial security important for the future needs of you and your family. A widely used rule of thumb is that you will need to replace 80 percent of your final earnings to maintain your standard of living after you retire. This percentage may have to be even greater in the future in order to take into account inflation, diminishing Social Security funds, the cost of post-retirement medical coverage and leisure activities.

Experts estimate that less than 20 percent of adults over the age of eighteen have a definite plan for retirement. Today is the day to take control of your financial future and declare your personal financial independence. The only person you can count on for your financial security is YOU. When you count on yourself, you are in control of your own circumstances, and with this control comes peace of mind. Also, thanks to the power of compound interest, the sooner you start saving the better. So get started today if you want to have a leisurely retirement. You will thank yourself in your old age! Therefore, with determination and perseverance, anyone can achieve financial independence. Here is a six-step plan to get you on the path towards financial independence.

1) Make a commitment and determine your priorities. The first step towards financial independence is making a commitment. Set a goal for yourself and then sign a personal declaration of financial independence as a reminder and motivator of your decision. Once you have made your commitment, establish your priorities. Determine what is important to you in life and begin to live out those principles that will enable you to achieve the financial independence you are seeking. Your financial priorities encompass many things such as education, basic necessities to survive, transportation, housing, et cetera. However, you must make decisions regarding how much you will spend on these priorities, and these decisions will determine how accurately you are following your path to financial independence. For example, you NEED a car to go to work, school, et cetera. Will you purchase a conservatively priced vehicle or will you overextend yourself financially and purchase the newest, most expensive SUV model? These are choices you must make continuously in order to decide if you are on the path towards your financial freedom. Once you set your priorities, design a plan to reach your goal.

2) Eliminate debt and establish a budget. For better or for worse, depending on your spending habits, credit has become a cornerstone of consumerism in our society today. In 2007, according to the Federal Reserve, Americans owed a combined $920 billion in revolving credit which is up from $748 billion in 2002. Debt is an American epidemic! Experts estimate that more than 75 percent of Americans are living in debt. Many do not see their income as a spending cap. About 43 percent of American families spend more than they earn, according to a Federal Reserve study. Experts estimate that on average Americans spend $1.22 for every dollar they earn. Most people are afraid to calculate their total debt for fear of the total being too much for them to carry. Therefore, many people are in denial regarding the total debt they owe. How will they ever be able to begin the process of paying down their debt if they are blind to the total sum? Knowledge is power! Do you know how much debt you are carrying? Calculate and know the exact amount of your debt so you can begin to make informed decisions regarding paying down your debt. Once you have analyzed your current debt to income ratio, find ways to pay down your debt as quickly as possible. Your options could range from borrowing money at a low interest rate to pay off high interest credit card debt; or stopping all other investments and using that money to bring your unpaid balance to zero; or making a drastic change, such as David and I did, like selling your house in order to begin living a debt free lifestyle. Look at what your present options are in regards to paying off your debt and make the appropriate decisions. Make sure that after each credit card is paid off, you cut up each card so that "history does not repeat itself." After you establish a plan for eliminating debt, create a budget and be determined to live within your means. At times, living within your means includes sacrificing a desire to indulge yourself. This can help you achieve your financial goals and stay debt free in the future.

3) Audit your finances. Once a month, sit down and take stock of your progress to date. Perform an audit each month on a different area of your finances. Review your spending pattern and make certain that your spending matches your priorities. You can refer back to Chapter 7 and utilize the chart on "needs vs. wants" in order to help you clarify whether your spending for that month was on needs or more on wants. Recalculate your debt to determine the impact of your debt elimination plan. Analyze your budget to see if it is still working for you. Lastly, look at your complete financial picture to view your financial puzzle as a whole instead of individual pieces.

4) Increase your financial IQ. Devote your free time to this endeavor because your life depends on it. From young adults to retirees, continued financial education is important. Increase your financial knowledge through a variety of outlets such as newspapers, financial books, seminars, Internet, et cetera. Learning about mutual funds, investment opportunities and a savings plan can diversify your finances and place you in a better financial position for the future.

5) Start thinking of the future. Now is the time to plan for your financial future by paying yourself first and setting up an emergency reserve. Each month, before you do anything else, place a set amount of money into a high yield savings or investment account. The concept of paying yourself first is one of the most effective ways to save and begin building a foundation for your financial security for the future. Also, since life is full of risks and financial pitfalls, begin building an emergency reserve. Experts advise to save between three and six months of living expenses in an easily accessible savings account. The amount of your reserve will depend on the flexibility of your budget and your comfort zone.

6) Resolve to stay on track. Take time to reassess your finances and your complete financial profile. Determine what has worked well and what you can improve on. Then reconfigure your financial plans to reflect the desired changes in your finances.

As you can see, it is extremely crucial for you to think about your future in regards to retirement. It is never too early to start saving for retirement. As mentioned previously, in order to maintain your current standard of living you will need close to 80 percent of your current income when you retire. This is a significant sum of money when you consider that Social Security may provide you with only about 25 percent of your income. How can you make up the other 55 percent of your income in order to maintain your current lifestyle? Here is a sneak preview of your options for retirement.

Individual Retirement Accounts (IRAs) make a great investment option. The two basic types of IRAs are Traditional IRAs and Roth IRAs. A Traditional IRA may give you an annual tax deduction (fully or partially). These earnings are tax-deferred. The maximum annual contribution for a Traditional IRA is $4,000 or 100 percent of earned income ($5,000 if 50 or older). The Roth IRA is a non tax-deductible IRA where your earnings can be distributed tax-free and penalty-free if certain conditions are met. The maximum annual contribution is $4000 or 100 percent of earned income ($5,000 if 50 or older).

There are even more options when you consider how you want your IRA invested. Numerous banks offer a variety of IRA Certificates for 6-, 12-, 18-, 24-, and 30-month terms. IRA Certificates offer a fixed rate for a specific term which gives you a predictable stream of income. There are also Investment IRAs. Investment IRAs have the potential to provide greater returns, depending on the length of time you plan to keep the IRA and your investment options. These funds are not federally insured and your principal may fluctuate.

You may also be eligible for a direct rollover with your IRAs. Do you have a retirement savings accumulating dust at a previous employer? If so, then consolidating all of your IRAs or retirement savings into one account will simplify your life. In the past, rolling a 403(b) or 457 plan into your new employer's 401(k) plan or even an IRA was not possible. However, current legislation now allows money in any of these plans to be transferred into a 401(k) or IRA. This legislation ultimately gives you more control over your financial investments.

If your employer offers you a matching contribution to a 401(k) retirement account, take him up on his offer. The maximum you can contribute in a 401(k) plan in 2007 is $15,500 ($20,500 if you are 50 or older). Even if you have debt, you should still divert some money into your 401(k) plan—at least enough to get the full company match. This will be money well spent for your retirement! If you do not take advantage of your company's offer to match your 401(k) contributions, you are basically turning away free money that would help you ultimately achieve your financial goals in the future. For example, money invested in your twenties and thirties has thirty to forty years to earn a positive cash flow return. However, if you wait until you are in your forties to start investing for retirement then that money only has about twenty years to grow. You will need to then put more money aside into your retirement account in order to achieve the same financial results as you would have had if saving began in your twenties. Saving for retirement early enough builds a substantial nest egg! For example if you start saving $5,000 a year (8 percent annual return) when you are twenty-five years old, then by the time you turn sixty-five you will have a comfortable amount of money, $1.3 million, to live off of. However, if you start saving twenty years later at the age of forty-five, then you will have less than $230,000 for retirement. That is a difference of more than a million dollars! Who can afford not to begin saving?

Now that you have taken an inventory of your financial assets and realized where you are in relation to where you want to be, what steps will you take in order to reach your financial goals? There are numerous incentives to save for your future such as financial stability, avoiding poverty, enjoying your golden years, et cetera. Which incentive speaks profoundly to the type of retirement you want for yourself? Whatever incentive you use, utilize it in order to tap into your strong desire for financial freedom, because ultimately that is what we all want in our retirement years. Use that incentive to get going and start saving for your retirement. It is wise to set realistic goals about your finances for the present and the future. In order to decide how much you plan to save for retirement, you need to decide how much you need for the present.

Chapter Sixteen

Are You Content?

The problem with living in an affluent and materially prosperous country is that we tend to draw our joy and happiness from that which we possess materially. Consequently, when we lack the vain things of this world, we are prone to become dissatisfied with life. Our dissatisfaction, as a society, is usually the result of comparison. This type of dissatisfaction is built on our constant mania to compare ourselves to others. Many people are unhappy in our society today because they are constantly looking around to see what everyone else has and what they personally are lacking. It is a constant game of who has acquired what and how I will strive to get those material possessions. Our society has lost the value and meaning of being content.

I looked up the word "content" in the Webster's dictionary and these are the definitions I retrieved: "satisfied; to limit oneself in requirements, desires or actions; feeling satisfaction with one's possessions, status or situation." To be content means to consume without gorging or hoarding possessions. Why is it so hard in our society today to feel content with what we have? Do we always have to keep up with the Jones's? The media further compounds this problem by having us buy into their idea that our external material possessions will dictate our level of contentment within. As a society, we are told that if we do not drive this type of car or own that luxurious house then we will not be happy and content with our present circumstances. The media is constantly bombarding us with messages such as, "You need this year's new model!"; or "You have got to get your hands on these new pair of jeans!"; or "Gotta get it! Gotta get it now!". These types of slogans seduce us into thinking that we have to buy that "thing." We are told by the media that if we do not attain these items then we are not good enough. Are we not people of worth without these material items? God created each and every one of us with unique skills and talents! Why do we buy into this lie of materialism in our society? A hundred years ago, people were not enticed by the materialism we are faced with today. They just did without and they didn't feel any less worthy or unhappy without all the big and expensive toys we make ourselves believe that we just have to have.

All of us are familiar with bank loans and credit card companies making it easier to satisfy our urges for instant gratification by the countless loans that are thrust our way. Through this practice, these institutions are "helping" us get deeper and deeper into debt. Every day the mail brings countless invitations offering pre-approved lines of credit. No wonder we are so easily lured in by these offers since they are so easily obtained. If we are not careful, we can be easily tempted to fill our world with material possessions and with no way of ever paying for them.

As a society, we are spending our way to financial disaster because we are attempting to satisfy the void within us with material possessions. This "void" is keeping us from being content with who we are and what we have. What then is the value of contentment? Being content could mean the difference between living a joyful and fulfilled life versus living a life of constant desire for material possessions and never feeling satisfied. In the Bible, the apostle Paul sets a good example for us on contentment in the following scripture: "…I have learned in whatever state I am, to be content" (Philippians 4:11). To give you some background, the apostle Paul was thrown in prison for his faith in God and not because of any wrongdoing on his part. While the apostle Paul was serving his time in prison, he began to write letters which describe how he had learned to be content with whatever circumstance he found himself. This realization for Paul was not an easy one, because his contentment brought its fair share of suffering and trials which he had to endure. The apostle Paul lived a joyful and fulfilled life because he learned how to be content by accepting the circumstances which God had placed in his life. Contentment is not an easy task to accomplish, but the rewards are great! Finding peace and joy in the midst of life's circumstances has wonderful benefits for those who dare seek His guidance.

In the Bible, God reveals to us that there are blessings in being content with what we have. In First Timothy 6:6-8, God says that "Godliness with contentment is great gain." Through these verses God is telling us that when we were born we came with nothing into this world and when we die we will not be able to take any of our material possessions with us. So why then do we fret over buying things we can not afford? As stated in these Biblical verses, we absolutely can not take these possessions with us to the grave! God clearly communicates to us that we need to be content if we have food to eat and clothes to wear. The term "clothes" here does not mean designer and expensive brands, but rather the bare necessities. Another verse is Luke 3:14 where God instructs us to be content with our wages. How many of us are constantly piping for the next raise? And when we finally do get that next raise, are we content? NO! We are again trying to climb that corporate salary ladder. There are numerous parables that Jesus gives in the Bible that relate to our finances. These Scriptures provide guidelines on how to manage our finances on a daily basis in order to honor God with our wages and also to be content with our circumstances.

Recently, David and I went to look at some open houses in order to see what the housing market has to offer us now and what we could afford based on our budget. As we began our search, I found myself walking through some of the more luxurious homes and saying things like "I want that fireplace" or "It would be so awesome to have that pool." We returned home later that day exhausted and inflated with wants and desires. The next day, David and I were talking and we both realized that we had let ourselves be enticed by the luxuries we saw. God brought to mind a scripture for us to ponder. This verse is in Hebrews 13:5 and it says to "...be content with what you have." We were reminded that we should be content with what we presently have! Through this verse, God also gently reminded us of how He has supplied our needs (though not necessarily every want!)

when our finances were especially tight. There were times when it was often a challenge to get a well-balanced meal on the table at the end of the month. However, God has always provided for our family even when the money didn't quite seem to stretch. God's provision has been evident every step of the way as we have sought his guidance and direction for our lives. In the next couple of years we would like to own a home again, but we know that we must choose wisely in order to continue our debt free lifestyle. David and I are attempting to daily abide by God's Biblical principles in regards to how we choose to manage our money. For now, we are prayerfully thankful that each month every need is met and every bill is paid on time. This to us is pure contentment! David and I daily strive to be content with what we have.

As Christians, David and I cherish our inward serenity and close relationship with God. In order for us to preserve this relationship, we must be content with our circumstances and know the difference between our actual needs and our frivolous wants. Jesus told us in Matthew 6:21 that "where your treasure is, there will your heart be also." We want to have our hearts directed in the right place which is heaven bound. David and I want to build heavenly treasure rather than earthly treasure where "thieves and moths" (Mathew 6:19) will destroy these material possessions. Where are you building your treasure? What financial strategies are you employing in order to become debt free, live a life of contentment and build heavenly treasure? These are tough questions to ponder.

Chapter Seventeen

Giving and Tithing

One way David and I are building heavenly treasure is by tithing every month. Tithing is the type of giving that is done in love and requires no audience. It springs from a deep spiritual relationship that puts God in the proper perspective as owner of all things. Psalm 24:1 states, "The earth is the Lord's and everything in it…" When we recognize that God owns everything (even our ability to work) our role as managers, or stewards, of our finances becomes evident. We are not "owners," but rather "managers" of our finances because "owner" implies that we can do as we please with the money we have earned. This is obviously not the case since God chooses to bless us with the ability to work and make money. Thus, the money is not ours, but rather it belongs to God. At the end of our days, we will be held accountable for the way we managed our finances.

Part of being a good manager or steward of our finances, is giving back to God a portion of what he has entrusted to us. It is not that God needs our money, but rather giving serves as an external testimony that God owns both the material and the spiritual things in our lives. One of the first standards of giving found in the Bible is the "tithe." The word tithe means a "tenth." God wants us to at least tithe (give) ten percent of our financial earnings to the church. Of course, you can always give more if you choose, but ten percent is the starting point that God has set forth for us.

If we want to be wise in handling our finances, we must seek wisdom from God. Proverbs 9:10 says, "The fear of the LORD is the beginning of wisdom..." One of the ways that God intends for us to do this is to acknowledge His Lordship by tithing. When we do not fear God, we discount His Lordship and put our will first. In the midst of this, we lose our eternal perspective, and the temporary worldly things gain importance in our lives. We begin to shift our attention to material possessions rather than to eternal treasures. For Christians, this bondage to worldly things often leads to calamities and ruined lives. Therefore, giving (tithing) is the only antidote to materialism. The act of giving is a concrete reminder that it is all about God and not about us. Giving breaks the chains of materialism that would otherwise enslave us.

God has asked us for our "firstfruits," (Deuteronomy 26: 1-2) not our leftovers. The firstfruits are the first and best of all that we receive financially. This means that we should tithe from our gross income. David and I have made it a priority to tithe 10 percent of our gross earnings to our church. As Christians, we believe that God requires us to put Him first in our financial planning.

The church we used to attend had a system set up where every month they would automatically deduct our tithe from our checking account. We had set up the withdrawal to coincide with the deposit of our paychecks. We designated an amount to tithe and every two weeks the church withdrew 10 percent of our earnings. The automatic tithe worked great for us because it helped us stay on track with our giving and it also dissipated any temptation we may have had in not tithing for that month. Of course, other churches might have a different setup in how they collect their tithes. Many churches prefer their congregation to manually write their checks and deposit them in the offering plate. There is no set standard in collecting the tithe. It is whatever works well for you and the method of collection of that corresponding church. The church we currently attend takes our tithe in the traditional manner. Every Sunday when the offering plate comes around, we "deposit" our tithe in the plate. For us this method, rather than the automatic withdrawal, takes a little more effort on our part because now we actually have to physically write the check, which then must be manually placed in the offering plate, but we are faithful nonetheless. Either way of tithing is acceptable to God as long as we are conscientious each month to give the firstfruits of our labor to God.

David and I also choose to donate our time to our church. There are various ministries that any given church offers. Based on your skills, talents and preferences, you can choose to serve in one position or various positions depending on your ability and time to serve. I have served in the children's ministry when my girls were younger and David has served as an usher on Sunday mornings. With my educational background, I have also tutored kids during the summer tutorial program at our church. As a couple, we have also served with our church in community outreach events. For example, during the Christmas season we purchased and wrapped gifts for those in our community who are less fortunate.. David and I have also filled shoe boxes with gifts and toys for kids during Christmas in order for the church to send these gifts to other countries where poverty runs rampant and children do not have the luxury of opening presents on Christmas morning. It is such a joy for us to participate in such events because we know that we are the hands and feet of Jesus here on earth. We are willing to be used by God to bless others!

There are numerous opportunities and organizations for all of us to become involved in by investing our time, talents and finances into the lives of others. One worthwhile organization that is dear to my heart is www.donorschoose.org. This organization assists teachers by providing them with classroom supplies they need in order to educate the next generation. I have experienced firsthand the personal time and financial resources teachers give to their classroom. With so many school districts experiencing tremendous budget cuts, teachers are the ones who ultimately have to fork out their funds in order to pay for basic classroom resources. Some of these resources include, but are not limited to pencils, erasers, crayons, paper, books, et cetera. These supplies, for the most part, need to be replenished on a yearly basis. Teachers spend an astronomical amount of money (their money) on classroom supplies without ever being reimbursed by the school district or the state. Teachers unselfishly give of themselves because they desire to see their students succeed. There are many teachers, however, who personally suffer financially due to the extensive classroom expenses they incur each year. These teachers have had to make do without some of the essential materials necessary for teaching their classroom because they simply did not have the funds to purchase school supplies. Unfortunately, there exists a scarcity of school supplies in our public school classrooms, and this scarcity negatively impacts the education of many children. Many teachers are looking towards other avenues such as donorschoose.org in order to fund their classroom supply lists and other educational projects.

This organization has a mission to ensure that teachers have the proper teaching materials to educate and that every student has access to the necessary supplies in order to achieve his/her optimal learning environment. Donorschoose.org enables citizens like you and me to participate in the generous funding of classroom needs for teachers across the country. This organization, as part of its mission statement, "envisions a nation where students in every community have the resources they need to learn." What an awesome opportunity to invest in the lives of children in our public schools! If you are interested in funding teacher supplies and projects, please visit their website. I guarantee that you will not be disappointed with how your financial contribution will impact students across the country. Experience the joy of giving children basic necessities such as books and pencils so many of us take for granted.

Another worthy organization which I heard about on the Oprah Winfrey show is called Kiva. Kiva.org is an online organization that makes small personal loans (with no interest) to low-income entrepreneurs in the developing world. Their motto is that by choosing an entrepreneur's business on Kiva.org, you can "sponsor a business and help the world's working poor make great strides towards economic independence." The way this organization works is that you go to your computer and log onto Kiva.org and their website appears. On Kiva's website you will see numerous individuals who are seeking your assistance. You as an individual have the power to act as a banker by lending a desired amount of your money to a person who is looking for a way out of poverty. What a great feeling knowing that you are giving someone a hand up rather than a hand-out! You can make a financial loan online through Kiva.org for the full amount of the loan or you can make a small donation for as little as $25. Any loan amount is gratefully received because other people in the United States who also know about this organization are also making financial loans to these individuals in the developing countries. Did you ever think that you could ever act as a banker for a person in need? Well, this is your opportunity to make loans to others and see their faithfulness in repaying their loans to you. What a testimony of trust! A loan is typically repaid in about six to twelve months. The majority of Kiva's entrepreneurs repay their loans in full; however, there is a low risk (0.4 percent) of unpaid loans. This low risk amount should not deter you from lending a helping hand to those in need. When your loan is paid in full by the borrower, it is then returned to you. Once you have received your original loan amount back, you then have two options. You can either take back your money or you can reinvest that loan into another business in order to assist another individual who is looking for a way out of the poverty stricken area he/she resides in. It is your money and it is your choice! What a great feeling knowing that you are empowering others to reach their goals and dreams by simply being a generous person and lending them money with no interest attached. Many third world entrepreneurs are looking to organizations such as Kiva to lend them the necessary funds because other institutions or individuals who are known to lend money in their country are known to attach a hefty interest on the entrepreneur's loan. Interest on an entrepreneur's loan can be as high as 35 percent. How can these entrepreneurs make it in these developing regions when they have to pay such a high interest on their loans? Obviously, it is very difficult to gain any sort of profit when one is hit with such outrageous interest rates. You are an angel in disguise when you offer your monetary assistance to others in need. Give Kiva.org a try and you will not regret it. David and I have made several loans to entrepreneurs on Kiva.org. What joy spills forth at the prospect of helping others! Knowing that we have the resources to enable others to fulfill their financial obligations by providing for their families and their communities gives us a better perspective of how important it is for us to make wise decisions regarding the financial resources with which we have been blessed. One day we will be held accountable by God for how we manage our finances. David and I want to reach the end of our journey in the presence of God and be told that we were wise stewards with the financial resources that God had entrusted to us here on earth. What a victorious day that will be!

As you can see, there are many opportunities for you to serve if you are willing to open up your heart, wallet and schedule. You are the only one who knows how much time and effort you are willing to set aside in order to serve others in need. Are you giving of yourself and your financial resources? Even if you are struggling to make ends meet, you still owe God what belongs to God. Even if you are in debt, you should still tithe and give your time to others. These offerings (whether monetary or service) we give to God help us "to fear God, which is the beginning of wisdom" the Bible states. The word "fear" in this verse does not imply feelings of harm or danger, but rather a reverence for who God is. If ever there is anyone in the world that needs God's wisdom in the area of finances, it is the person who is in debt. Therefore, trust God in the area of your finances by tithing and serving others and then watch to see how God chooses to bless you because you were obedient to His word.

Chapter Eighteen

Kids and Money

Since David and I are so adamant about tithing and saving, we also want to instill these fundamental qualities in our kids. We want our kids to know that the financial resources they are blessed with come from God and that the fruits of their labor are blessed because they honor God first by tithing.

Our daughters are old enough (Amanda – ten and Allison – eight years old) to understand the tithing and saving principle, but our son is only a toddler. In time, however, we plan to also teach him the value of these fundamental issues. Teaching our kids about money was no easy task, but David and I knew that they are now old enough to grasp the money concept. This is how our story began. Every time David or I would go shopping, our daughters used to ask us to buy them this or that toy. They seemed to think that money really did grow on trees since there was no end in sight for things they wanted to purchase. From time to time, David and I would give in and buy them the toy they wanted, but we were later disappointed when the next day we would find that new toy at the bottom of the toy box. That new toy had lost its newness and now the girls had their eye out for other "new" toys they wanted to buy. David and I were tired of dishing out money for the toys the girls were always begging us to buy for them. We also realized that the girls did not have any concept regarding how hard we had worked to gain those monetary funds used to purchase their toys.

David and I decided that the girls needed to learn the value of money.

We decided to give the girls a small allowance each month for age appropriate chores around the house in order to teach them the concept of acquiring and maintaining monetary funds. This concept has revolutionized the 'money battles" in our home. Let me clarify: the girls used to beg and argue with us in order to break us down and purchase that new toy or gadget. David and I were so tired of bargaining and finally getting so angry and saying a flat out "NO" to our daughters, which then would send the girls into a "tantrum" mode. Now with their monthly allowance, Amanda and Allison are now able to decide for themselves whether or not they want to spend their money on that particular toy or if they want to save their money. We informed the girls that if they save their money instead of spending it on every toy they see, they will be able to accumulate a larger amount of cash that they can either spend on a bigger toy, or they can save. David and I wanted to let the girls begin making decisions with their money so they can learn the value of a dollar.

When Amanda and Allison were seven and five, respectively, David opened a savings account for each of them. The girls know that they have a safe and secure place to store their money. Amanda and Allison are now saving more of their money and making discretionary purchases on their own. The girls also know that any money they receive for their birthdays or Christmas must be saved in their savings account and not spent. When they accumulate a substantial amount of money, David and I match their contributions dollar for dollar in order to encourage them to keep on saving. After Amanda and Allison have doubled their money, we take the girls to the bank to deposit the accumulated cash into their savings account. We want to teach our daughters that every penny saved does amount to a larger sum of money. The purpose of our physically taking Amanda and Allison to the bank to deposit their own money into their savings account is for them to see that saving their money yields interest and that interest adds to their growing savings account. We informed the girls that when their savings account reaches a certain amount, we will take their hard earned dollars and place the funds in a higher yielding CD account so they can further see their money grow. Another reason we take the girls to the bank is to instill in them that this is a better alternative to their money rather than spending it all and being left with nothing but junk at the bottom of their toy box. These resourceful habits, we hope, will last a lifetime for our daughters!

We have taught our daughters to tithe 10 percent of the allowances they receive. David and I want our girls to know that God is blessing them with these financial resources and they need to be obedient by giving of their firstfruits to the Lord. Tithing teaches the girls to obey and trust God with their lives. As our children get older and begin working at their first job, we want to teach them to continue tithing (10 percent) and saving (10 percent) from each paycheck in order to further reinforce these essential habits for a lifetime.

As our girls are learning the skills necessary for money management as youngsters, we hope that these values will be beneficial as they mature and begin making wise choices about their spending and saving habits. For example, we have told them that a sale in a store is not a sale if they cannot afford to pay for it with cash. The reason we tell Amanda and Allison this is because David and I do not want to see our kids enslaved by debt like we were. Our family's motto is, "Earn some, tithe some, save some and spend some." We hope this motto teaches our kids that earning money comes with responsibility. This responsibility encompasses how they respond to God, save for their future and play with their money. Yes, we even teach our kids how to enjoy their money responsibly. We want our girls to know that spending their hard earned funds can also be fun and entertaining and not just burdensome. David and I want to consistently show our kids that there are some hard lessons to learn regarding money management, but there are also rewards that come with self-control in handling their finances. Our daughters learn the art of money management by watching us handle the delicate balance of earning, tithing, saving and spending our money. David and I hope to be positive role models for our kids to emulate as they are seeking to handle their own monetary funds.

Who were your role models for money management as a youngster? If we were honest with ourselves, most of us would have to say our parents were the primary adults who introduced us to the concept of money. Managing finances is something many of our parents never taught us how to do. It seems that all we ever saw was an inconsistency our parents exhibited since we heard them saying one thing about money and yet doing the exact opposite with their finances. As we now parent our own children, we need to become intentional about the way in which we communicate finances to our kids. Our children need to hear and see us doing the things we are preaching to them rather then contradicting ourselves in front of them. For example, since you are encouraging your children to save money, do they also see you going to the bank to deposit funds into the family's savings account? Your actions and words about money should be consistent because your kids are watching your every move. If you say one thing but do another, your child will see through this hypocrisy very quickly. On the other hand, consistency will reinforce all of your efforts and what you say will support what you do and vice versa.

For most of us parents, the topic of money is a big subject to teach our kids. However, money education is focused on four basic principals. They are **earning money**—putting in personal time and effort to receive payment; **saving money**—setting aside money today so that it will be there in the future; **spending money**—using money that has been earned or saved to pay for things; and **borrowing money**—using money that will have to be repaid in the future at more than what was originally received. These four simple yet essential strategies could be the basic building blocks of how we as parents begin introducing and educating our children about this complex subject called money management. A concrete example of how you may want to begin teaching your children about money is to purchase piggy banks for them. Young kids need this tried and true symbol of saving. Children should know that there is an object in which to deposit and save pocket change if they do not spend it. Many kids view money as an abstract topic because they see their parents using credit cards and also banking online. Kids hardly ever get to see the cold hard cash being utilized because of how technology is enabling parents to electronically manage money. Children desperately need to grasp this concept that money really is a concrete object which you can physically touch and manage in person.

Our daughters learned the lesson of how concrete money really is when they saw their grandpa place everyday pocket change into a Sparkletts water canister. My father-in-law had been collecting spare pocket change for several years in this empty jug. In the summer of 2007, Amanda and Allison had informed their grandparents that they had a savings account in which they were saving their money for college expenses. When they heard this, my mother-in-law decided to pour a small amount of change from the jug into a bag for each of the girls so they could further their funds for college. Later that week, I took my daughters to a local grocery store where they have this machine called Coinstar. This machine takes your change and electronically calculates the amount of money you have and then gives you a receipt. You then take this receipt to the cash register and the cashier then hands you the amount of money specified on that receipt. After both Amanda and Allison completed this transaction, they each received $60 cash. They were so amazed that so little pocket change can amount to big bucks! My girls received a great concrete lesson of how saving spare change amounts to big savings. We then, of course, immediately went to the bank and deposited the $60 into each of their savings accounts. There is more, however, to the story of the infamous money jug. The next weekend, my husband, his younger brother and our girls took the rest of the money jug and went to the local grocery store to cash in the rest of the change using the Coinstar machine again. Amanda and Allison were again shocked to see that just mere pocket change can add up to over $1000 in cold hard cash! That's right! There was $1100 in that jug of just pocket change that had accumulated over several years. Our daughters saw their grandpa with ten $100 bills and some $20 bills. What a great testament of money saved! In total, my father-in-law had collected a little over $1200 of spare change (counting the $120 he previously gave our girls). My in-laws took their pocket change (over $1000) on their cruise as spending money! Amanda and Allison were grateful to their generous grandparents for giving them an additional $40 each for their hard work in cashing in the rest of the money jug. Guess what the girls did with the extra cash? Yep, they deposited into their savings accounts. Imagine what spare change can add up to!

As you can see, we need to provide our children with great role models of how to effectively manage finances because this is one subject they will not be taught at school. As our children age, we need to adjust the conversation about money to the next level. For example, as kids become teenagers, they want more autonomy with their spending money. As parents, we need to match their trust with the accountability factor. Kids need to know that they will be held accountable in regards to how they chose to spend their funds, and they also need to know that there will be consequences for their actions if they are not responsible with their spending. For example, if your teenage son or daughter spends all of his/her allowance before the next payday, you as the parent have three options in this case. You can either let them suffer the consequences of going without the "extras" for the remainder of the month until the next payday; just give in and use your money to purchase their wants; or you can teach them the concept of borrowing money from you. You have to ask yourself what lesson you want to teach your child in regards to money management. If you choose to give in and use your funds, then you are teaching your child that Mom and Dad will be here whenever you need to be bailed out of future financial disasters. However, if you choose to lend your child money, then they will become familiar with the concept of borrowing and paying interest on the funds they utilize. As we all know, borrowing money from a bank usually entails promising to repay the loan by signing your name on the dotted line, setting up a repayment plan and deciding on an interest rate for the repayment of the loan. You as the parent can decide how far you want your teenage son or daughter to experience the challenging decisions and responsibility that come with repaying a debt. You, as the parent, are teaching and enabling your child to experience the hardships and responsibilities associated with money management. You are giving your child the opportunity to succeed and fail under your guidance and leadership.

David and I are modeling the act of saving for our children by contributing monthly to a 529 Plan. We have told our children that we are putting money away each month for each of them in order to ensure a debt free life for them when they graduate from college. A Section 529 Plan is basically a college savings account. We all know that college expenses are rising at an astronomical rate, and the 529 Plan allows us to plan strategically and effectively for college. I love this savings plan because it is automatically deducted from our gross pay each month without our giving it a second thought. Another great benefit to the 529 Plan is that these funds are taken out federally tax-free. This means that as long as the money in the 529 savings plan is used for college related expenses then the money is not taxed. What a great way to use our money effectively—saving for college and not being taxed on the money we contribute to the account! The 529 plan allows us to prepare financially for college expenses our children will incur.

We did some research on what the 529 plans entails and this is what we found out. The 529 Plans are state sponsored savings programs designed to pay for college expenses. The term "expenses" refers to tuition, room and board, books, and required supplies and equipment needed for college. There are many benefits to a 529 Plan such as tax-free earnings growth:

- contributions are taken out of your paycheck before taxes;
- tax-free distributions for qualified education expenses—meaning that as long as the funds are allocated for college related expenses then you can withdraw the money tax-free;
- simplified and flexible rollover between 529 Plans—most states have turned over the operation of the plan to money management firms like Fidelity, Merrill-Lynch, Salomon Smith-Barney, et cetera, who market the plans on a nationwide basis and thus allows the easily transferable funds from one firm to another;
- the control of the account stays with the account owner and not the beneficiary—this allows you to monitor the withdrawn expenses to ensure that your child(ren) actually uses the 529 funds for college related expenses only;
- current maximum contribution limit up to $265,000—you can contribute to this savings account up to a maximum amount of $265,000;

- the 529 Plan can fund many post-secondary programs for the beneficiary—bachelor's, master's and PhD programs.

As you can see, there are many benefits to opening up a college savings account for each of your children. What a great way to ensure that your children graduate debt free from college! They will be grateful for the opportunity to plan for the future rather than attempting to pay off their student debts for many years.

Our children deserve to be taught common sense and caution when it comes to money. We need to be our children's teachers in order to educate, motivate and empower our kids to become regular savers and investors. These critical skills and strategies which we are attempting to instill within our kids will enable them to keep more of the money they earn and do more with the money they are spending. Communicating with our kids about money gives us, as parents, the opportunity to enlighten them about what the most important things in life really cost! We are building a lifelong legacy when we invest in our kids.

Chapter Nineteen

Leaving a Legacy

There is a deep curiosity inside every human being to peer into the depths of another human's soul in order to examine his/her life in hopes of finding unique treasures that will give us guidance and direction for our own lives. What causes this spark of interest? What draws us to examine and emulate the behaviors of another? The reason is simple. We all long for a legacy. Our joyful reward for peeking into another's life would be to find a little piece of history hiding there. A legacy is timeless! It reflects the heart and motives of the person who left it and brings joy and inspiration to those blessed to have found it.

A legacy, once found, helps each of us to decide the kind of life we want to live and the kind of world we want to live in. When you start thinking about your legacy you begin to take note of your possessions, accomplishments and disappointments. You take stock of what you have learned from what you have done in the past, what you are doing now, and what you still hope to do. You inevitably begin to reflect on the people, work, and commitments that have given your life shape and meaning. Therefore, legacies are about life and living. They are about learning from the past, living in the present, and building for the future.

Leaving a legacy is so important! Every one of us leaves a legacy. Your very existence has an impact on the world whether you intend for it to or not. So, how do you want to be remembered? What do you want your children and grandchildren to say about you once you are gone? The choices you make every day with your time and your finances directly impact those around you, especially your family. In fact, you have the ability to influence future generations so that even after you die, your legacy will continue to invest in their lives until the end of time.

Many Christians today, unfortunately, forget that God owns everything, and they live as if this world is their permanent home. Christians need to examine the basic assumptions about the place of money in our lives. We are living today in a time of unprecedented wealth and luxury. However, we seem to give little thought to money management either because of fear due to the debt we have accumulated or just pure negligence in handling our finances. Due to this fear or negligence, many people are leaving bleak legacies of financial chaos. A great deal of this financial chaos is due to the overwhelming burden of debt to which they are enslaved. Their bondage to debt has debilitated them from finding peace, joy and fulfillment in life. This overwhelming debt has become an all-consuming and encompassing force in their lives. We have all heard the saying, "He who dies with the most toys wins." However, are you aware that, "He who dies with the most toys is nonetheless still dead"? As a society, we cannot seem to understand that when we die, we cannot take our material possessions with us. All of our "stuff" remains here on earth. So why do we work so hard in order to buy all the up-to-date gadgets and expensive must-haves? We obviously cannot take these material possessions with us to the grave, but we are so determined, for whatever reason, to acquire these vain things. We must, therefore, reexamine our obsession with our frivolous spending habits.

A person's spending habits reveal his values. What are values, you ask? Values are the cornerstone ideals about what you believe is good or bad and right or wrong. These foundational ideals guide and direct your journey in life. You must, therefore, know what your values are before you can know how much money will bring you financial independence. For example, do you value material comfort, fairness, wealth, competition, individualism, religious liberty, justice, et cetera? As you can see, values play an important role in shaping who we are. Many people, unfortunately, fail to examine their values deeply and often follow the crowd in money management decisions which inevitably leaves them flat broke and in debt. For example, how many of us have not gone out and bought the newest must-have gadgets or toys because everyone else had them? Even though we really didn't need another pair of jeans or that new SUV, we felt compelled to purchase such items since we are keeping up with the Jones's. We must reevaluate our current spending habits and make lifestyle changes in order to free up funds for use in areas that really matter such as saving and investing. Wise money management involves finding a balance between proper enjoyment of the present and thoughtful provision for the future. Too much enjoyment of the present leads to a financially difficult future. Many people today are living for the moment and not giving their future a second thought. Americans need to break free from the bondage of debt that has enslaved them in the present and strapped them financially for the future. People need to find a balance for their finances by tailoring their spending habits in order to achieve their financial goals.

How would you fill in this blank: "If I died today, my legacy would be..."? If you are not sure how to complete this sentence, here are some thoughts for you to ponder: "What would people say about me? How have I helped others? Did I use my finances wisely? Was God honored through my finances? Did my life have meaning and purpose? Was I generous with my financial resources?" These are all questions that will define the legacy you leave behind, whether intentional or not.

It is important to remember that a person's generosity reveals his heart's motives towards money. A person's legacy will reveal his true intentions in life by how generous he was towards others with his financial resources. God uses generosity in our lives not only to bless others, but to also help us relinquish our greedy hold on money. In First Timothy 6:10, God talks about how "the love of money is the root of all kinds of evil." When we focus on money alone, then we are tempted to become greedy with our material possessions. However, when we transfer our attention towards others and fulfill their tangible needs which may otherwise go unmet, then we are learning to relinquish the greedy hold that money has in our lives. When we give generously out of joy and thanksgiving, it is then and only then that we experience God's abundant blessings. The Bible teaches that God's blessings (which are not always material ones) are bestowed upon his children who: are obedient; help the poor; pray and give; are merciful; keep His commandments; and are blessed for no other reason than pure grace. We need to become excited about investing our time, talent, and financial resources God has given us into the lives of others, so that one day we will hear Him say, "Well done, good and faithful servant" (Matthew 25:21). Since the true owner of all our resources is God, we will one day give an account for the management of those resources He has entrusted to us. Therefore, we need to be wise and use discernment in handling our financial resources.

Americans are known for their love of shopping whether they can afford it or not. Some experts compare consumerism in our society today to substance abuse. Like substance abuse, breaking the spending habit is an addiction many Americans just cannot live without. This consumer-driven mentality has jeopardized the present and financial future of many families. If you are not able to independently tackle your debt, then you need to seek out counsel from trained financial experts regarding managing and budgeting your finances, getting and staying out of debt, saving, and investing. By consulting with financial experts, you will be able to gain control over your finances rather than letting the financial crisis dictate your life. Therefore, in today's fast-paced world, each of us must learn how to manage our finances to ensure that our efforts are directed toward goals of lasting value.

Are you building a lasting legacy? We must be intentional of the legacy we leave behind. Working towards a legacy keeps you motivated and performing at your peak. It gives a higher purpose to your life. Your life will have an edge and energy because you are no longer "just living;" you are building a legacy. Above all, it helps you share the fullest of who you were meant to be with others. Another benefit about building a meaningful legacy is that money will eventually lose its grip on your heart as you learn to budget accordingly, learn the grace of generosity and practice giving in faith. What steps are you taking to leave behind a lasting legacy?

You cannot underestimate the importance of leaving a worthwhile legacy for future generations. We all have a responsibility to lead our lives in such a way that our children will be left with an unshakable legacy. The legacy we leave behind will be the foundation on which our children and grandchildren will build their lives upon. Children have a deep longing to see that their parents were responsible with the resources that God had entrusted to them while on this earth. As parents, our faithfulness in handling our finances today speaks volumes to future generations after we die about what was important to us during our brief journey here on earth.

David and I want to leave a stable and fruitful legacy for our children. We do not want our kids to remember their lives as one of financial instability, fear and overwhelming debt. Our children need to know that living within our means is not a punishment, but rather a lifestyle God intended for us to live by. David and I are being intentional about the legacy we leave behind for future generations. By God's grace, we hope our legacy will speak volumes about our generosity, faithfulness and financial stewardship.

Chapter Twenty

Conclusion

It has taken me two-and-a-half years to write this book. What a journey this has been! God has given me insight and wisdom into how David and I have handled our family's finances. It has not been easy to reflect upon our financial detours, but it has been rewarding to see the fruits of our labor. We have had to make numerous sacrifices along the way such as renting instead of buying, our daughters changing schools several times, leaving our church, et cetera. However, through all of our sacrifices we have accomplished our goal of eliminating our debt. This decision has enabled us to break free from the bondage of being enslaved to our creditors. We have obeyed God's commandment to owe no one anything but the obligation to love one another. What a feeling of freedom we have!

The act of sacrifice seems to be a foreign concept in our society today. Society's motto seems to be "give it to me now" instead of later! Delayed gratification is an art of the past. To live debt free in a society consumed with material possessions is a foreign concept to many Americans. The excessive need in our society to acquire material possessions has robbed many families of joy and contentment. For example, listen to some of the clichés Americans are buying into: "Buy a new couch for nothing down and no payments for year!" "Buy a new $600,000 house for a monthly payment of only $1200!" These enticing deals sound so great that we forget to read the fine print when we sign away our lives on the dotted line. Buying a new couch for no money down sounds like an incredible deal; however, have we thought about a year in advance and how we are going to pay for this furniture when we are already strapped financially with other debt? How about that new house we have purchased with the low mortgage payment? The mortgage seems affordable now with the three-year interest only loan, but how about when it readjusts to the current interest rate? Will you still be able to truly afford your house? Most Americans are making financial decisions based on their short-term views rather than thinking long-term about the purchases they are making. Many people have strapped themselves financially for the future in order to gain temporary enjoyment for the present. If you find yourself in this predicament, then you need to think long and hard about the sacrifices you now need to make in order to gain control of the financial chaos you created.

Making financial and lifestyle sacrifices is important and worthwhile in order to obtain what you really want out of life. You have to make a conscious decision about the life you want to lead. Do you want a life where debt, arguments, and late fees rule the way you live, or do you want a life full of joy and contentment? It is your decision. It takes hard work, dedication, patience and sacrifice in order to attain your financial goals of becoming debt free. However, in the end what you really want to have (financial freedom) is attainable if, and only if, you are willing to give up this culture's obsession with instant gratification and save your money in order to pay cash for your purchases. Saving your hard earned money will then enable you to avoid using your credit cards which put you in this bind in the first place. Therefore, having a savings plan in place will allow you to pay for those unforeseen expenses in cash rather than with credit. Strategic financial planning and saving allows you to be in charge of your money instead of depending on credit cards to always bail you out when life happens.

I have heard many people say that they just cannot save any money because they are so financially strapped. I used to say the same thing when we were in debt over our heads, but looking back now, I see some of the frivolous spending on my part. Those frivolous funds could have gone into our savings account. Therefore, every one of us can save money if we really look for ways to cut back on our expenses. We can all begin saving small increments of cash starting with even a dollar. Remember my story about my father-in-law saving his pocket change and then all of a sudden he had accumulated over a thousand dollars in cash. We can all start somewhere to save because saving starts with pocket change, or if we have the cash we can allocate more funds towards savings.

It pains me to hear families say that they are living paycheck to paycheck, but in their home they have a new plasma TV. Was this purchase a need or a want? Obviously this expense is certainly a want. Many families are also saying that they are having a difficult time paying their bills, but in their driveway they have the latest SUV that has just been leased. Again, is this a reasonable need or is this a want? I think you know the answer to this one. You have to decide if you really want that new expensive handbag or do you need to put food on the table for that month? It is all about making sacrifices and choices about paying the bills, feeding your family, leasing an expensive car, et cetera. Therefore, the next time you feel like you are experiencing difficulty making ends meet, then reflect upon where every last dollar has gone for the last month. You will be amazed at the findings!

By the grace of God, my family and I have been able to make the necessary sacrifices in order to embrace the debt free lifestyle we are now living. What a relief we have experienced as a family by not being enslaved by our creditors. David and I used to spend many sleepless nights worrying if we would be able to pay our bills and put food on the table. Now, by God's grace, we are able to peacefully lay our heads down at night and not worry that our creditors will come knocking on our doors to demand their payments. We are by no means rich, but David and I have learned to live within our means. This implies that if we do not have the cash to purchase necessities, then we do without. This may seem harsh to some, but to our family it has given us the privilege and opportunity to enjoy life without any strings attached to any creditors. What a blessing! Also, another incredible benefit of being debt free is that our marriage has become the type of partnership where love and respect are mutually reciprocated between David and me. We are no longer fighting over financial matters, but rather we are communicating with one another about our financial spending and future goals. Marriage has become a wonderful partnership rather than just a relationship to sustain.

Another benefit of being debt free is that David and I have realized that by giving of ourselves and our finances (tithing) we have released the control that material possessions used to have in our lives. Material possessions no longer control us, but rather we are in control of how we choose to allocate our funds. David and I have also realized that giving of our time and tithing are acts of obedience on our part towards God. God commands us to tithe and give of ourselves to Him and others. Giving and tithing releases the servanthood attitude in us rather than hoarding the greed monster we all posses within ourselves. Tithing and giving allows us the privilege to serve others with a humble heart. However, money is not all we can give. Time, wisdom and expertise are also wonderful gifts to share with others. Giving in any form breaks "affluenza's" fever. The act of giving and tithing breaks us from the gravitational hold of money and possessions.

If you also want to break affluenza's fever in your own life, then this is a great time to start reevaluating your finances. Are you struggling to make ends meet? Are you striving to achieve a debt free lifestyle? Are you learning to tithe more regularly and give of your time and expertise to others? Then I urge you to begin your journey toward financial freedom by breaking free from the chains of bondage that are keeping you enslaved to your debt. This path you are embarking upon is not an easy one, but it is well worth the effort once you have achieved your goal of being debt free. Remember that you didn't get into debt overnight and therefore you will need to take baby steps to achieve your financial goals. If you feel overwhelmed by your financial circumstances, take incremental steps to begin attacking your debt. Remember that eliminating your debt is not an overnight phenomenon. If you have attempted to resolve your financial crisis on your own but are having difficulty with the process, then seek professional credit counseling. There are trained professionals who are willing to rescue you from the mound of debt in which you have buried yourself. These professionals will get the collection agencies off your back and put you back on the right path towards correcting your credit problems.

Whether you decide to tackle your financial problems on your own, like we did, or you seek out professional credit counseling, you owe yourself the privilege to regain control of your life again.

When you are in debt, your creditors dictate how you live your life. Let me explain: your creditors control your life from how you allocate every penny to all those sleepless nights you encounter night after night. You are spending every waking moment attempting to figure out how you will repay all your debts without losing your home, your job, your family (divorce), and most of all, your sanity. Don't you want relief from this stressful lifestyle? Don't you want peace of mind knowing that your past debts are repaid and your recurring bills are paid on time? I know that deep down you want this financial chaos to end. You want peace and financial stability to prevail in your life. What a day of rejoicing this will be when you are indeed debt free!

I can assure you from experience that becoming debt free took a lot of determination, sacrifice and perseverance. Our intentional efforts to become debt free were worth the sacrifices we endured along the way. The tremendous financial load we were carrying has been lifted off our shoulders and now we can focus on giving, saving, tithing and investing our time rather than focusing on repaying old debt. David and I have changed our financial outlook from a bleak perspective about the future to one of hope and anticipation. By the grace of God, we will continue to remain debt free and optimistic about the financial choices we make for our family. David and I have broken free from the bondage of debt to which we were enslaved, and we hope and pray that this cycle of debt stops from perpetuating itself in our lives and in the lives of our children. Therefore, we are preventing future debt by being intentional about the financial choices we are making in order to avoid any financial catastrophes in the future.

Chapter Twenty-one

Reflections

The privilege of motherhood has been one of the greatest gifts that God has bestowed upon me. I love being a mom! One of my desires after becoming a parent was to spend more time at home with my children. As written previously, due to the overwhelming amount of debt we had accumulated, I had to work in order to pay off our creditors. Over the last two-and–a-half years of living debt free, I have been able to fulfill my dream of being home more with my children. I now work part time as a substitute teacher. I take the girls to school and then I fulfill my day-to-day substituting job. Then when my kids are done with school, I am also done with work and I pick them up from school. Instead of putting my kids in daycare for someone else to rear, I have the privilege of rearing my dear children. What a treasured gift this has been for me! Since David and I are committed to living a debt free life, the rewards have been numerous, especially allowing me to spend more time raising our daughters. Our third child was born six months ago and we decided to have me stay home for his first year. By the grace of God, we are able to budget and live within our means. I have to tell you that it has been challenging living off of one income and debt free in Southern California, but the financial sacrifices we have had to make have been well worth the effort.

Through these financial endeavors David and I have undertaken, we have had the privilege and honor to rely upon each of our parents for support, guidance and direction. Each set of parents has helped us throughout the last ten years with babysitting; giving financial assistance during our emergencies; entertaining our children; helping us pack and unpack several times during our moves; praying for us on a daily basis; and in contributing so many more tangible and intangible gifts. David and I are blessed and grateful for the love and leadership that our parents have generously given to us.

I am so blessed to have such wonderful in-laws! Over the last eleven years that David and I have been married, I have watched them successfully manage the financial resources which God has entrusted to them. My mother and father-in-law have worked hard for the last thirty years to save their money for retirement, put three boys through college, pay off two mortgages on two separate houses, and faithfully tithe and serve in their church. What great role models they have been for us! David and I strive to emulate their work ethic, financial resourcefulness, and their faithful service to God. It has been an honor and a privilege to walk alongside them all of these years. Thank you, Mom and Dad, for being wonderful role models! Congratulations on your forty-fifth wedding anniversary!

I have to tell you that I am also proud of my mom and dad for repaying their overwhelming amount of debt they had owed. Remember me telling you at the beginning of this book that my parents came to this country from Romania with just the "shirts on their back"? Literally! We couldn't even bring our suitcases my parents had packed. Romanian immigration forced us to leave our luggage behind. The only thing my mom and dad brought over to the US was a grocery bag packed with a few sandwiches and snacks for us to eat on our long trip. Obviously we lacked much in basic necessities, so my parents had to take out several loans and utilize several credit cards over the years in order to make ends meet.

As a child, we lived a very poor lifestyle. We lived in a two-bedroom apartment until I left home to attend college and my dad drove his hatchback, brown Pinto for years. My parents had accumulated $25,000 in debt in order to provide us with the bare necessities. This amount of debt is enormous for anyone, but it is especially challenging for an immigrant family to repay such a large amount of money on a very limited income. It would have been very easy for my parents to declare bankruptcy, but they knew deep down that this easy way out was not the answer for them. By the grace of God, my parents were faithful to repay every creditor they ever borrowed from. I know that this endeavor, however, was not easy for my parents, and they made a great deal of sacrifices to eradicate their overwhelming burden of debt. One of these sacrifices has been that they have never been able to own a home in the twenty-five years that they have lived in the United States. My parents were always so determined to pay off their debt that they decided that owning a house would further put them into debt that they may not be able to repay. I believe that God was honored by their efforts to do the right thing with their finances. Thank you, Mom and Dad, for enduring the sacrifices you have made in order to achieve a debt free life. You are great role models for David and me. God has been honored in your efforts to do the right thing.

Like my parents, since David and I have been intentional about freeing ourselves from the chains of bondage that enslaved us, God has been faithful in His provision for our family. He has given us our basic necessities such as food, shelter, health, et cetera, but God has also given us "a peace that surpasses all understanding." God's faithful provision for our family encompasses our physical, emotional, spiritual and financial needs. God has been faithful to provide for our every need and not always for our every want, but that is OK because we know that His plan for our lives is much bigger than we can ever imagine. Throughout this journey of becoming debt free, David and I have learned to trust God with our finances. We are now able to tithe monthly from our gross income and trust that God will provide for our needs each month. I have to tell you, though, that trusting God is not always easy. Sometimes I think to myself, *"How can we survive financially this month after we tithe,"* but God has been faithful. I have watched God take our very last dollar and stretch it to miraculous ends that I could never have imagined. We have even witnessed God use our family and friends to bless us with some of the needs we had. What a testament to God's faithful provision for our family! One of our prayers and financial goals is that God will provide a house that fits within our financial budget. David and I want to continue our debt free lifestyle forever. We want to leave a lasting legacy to our children, grandchildren and to future generations of what it looks like to be good stewards of the financial resources God has entrusted to us.